EASY TO MAKE

CRESCENT BOOKS
NEW YORK • AVENEL

First published in Great Britain in 1994 by
Anaya Publishers Ltd, London.

This 1995 edition published by Crescent Books,
distributed by Random House Value Publishing, Inc.,
40 Engelhard Avenue, Avenel, New Jersey 07001

Random House
New York • Toronto • London • Sydney • Auckland

Design and photography: Patrick McLeavey

A CIP catalog record for this book is available from the
Library of Congress.

ISBN 0–517–12147–6

Typeset by Bookworm Typesetting, Manchester
Color reproduction by Scantrans Pte Ltd, Singapore
Printed and bound in Portugal by Printer Portuguesa Lda

NOTES
All spoon measures are level.

Use fresh herbs and freshly ground black pepper
unless otherwise stated.

Use standard AA or A large eggs, unless otherwise
suggested.

Throughout this book "Preparation time" refers to the time required
to prepare the ingredients. It does not include time for cooking,
soaking, marinating, etc., which is given in the recipe method.

CONTENTS

Salads have become increasingly innovative and international over the years, with the growing choice of ingredients available. With so many unusual salad and herb leaves featuring on our supermarket shelves, the salad lover has a constantly growing source of inspiration for creating new salads.

Add to this leafy base the huge variety of other vegetables, beans, meats, cheeses, seafoods, fruits and nuts available to us, and you can create an infinite number of salads to suit every taste and occasion.

Most salads make for healthy eating because, whatever you add to them, their basic ingredients are raw vegetables that retain their vitamins and minerals. These being water-soluble, would otherwise be lost in cooking. Raw food generally, and ingredients like nuts and dried fruit in particular, also help to provide the fiber necessary for a healthy diet.

For the health-conscious, *Easy to Make Salads* contains chapters on fresh and healthy salads, and grains, beans and pasta. The eleven *Fresh and Healthy* recipes use light dressings and ingredients such as fruit, tofu and low-fat fromage blanc and yogurt. The twelve salads based on *Grains, Beans and Pasta,* while not necessarily low in calories, are high-fiber recipes which can be eaten as meals in themselves.

Salad days do not necessarily spell "D-I-E-T." Nor do they have to end with the onset of winter. *Easy to Make Salads* contains recipes that can be enjoyed in every season, whether you are counting calories or being a little self-indulgent. Besides classic favorites such as *Salade Niçoise* and *Caesar Salad* and some unusually-dressed side salads, you can try original main courses like *Crispy Duck and Mango Salad* or go for something spicy and exotic like *Bombay Salad*, a combination of zucchini and blanched broccoli with toasted cashews and coconut, finished with a curry-flavored dressing.

Much fresh produce, despite year-round availability, is still best in its proper season. For example, try *Salad Elona* in early summer when strawberries are at their best both in flavor and value for money. *Summer Herb and Flower Salad* is a visually stunning salad, an ideal choice for summer months when fresh herbs, varied salad leaves and edible summer flowers, such as borage, are plentiful. Similarly, use abundant pears in autumn to make *Pear, Stilton and Walnut Salad.* Other recipes, like *Chickpea and Chorizo Sausage Salad* or *Gadoh-Gadoh,*

which use dried, storecupboard or exotic ingredients, will taste just as good the whole year-round.

Whether using seasonal or storecupboard ingredients, it is essential for these to be of high quality. This is especially true when preparing simple, easy-to-cook recipes and when, as in this book, many ingredients are used raw. Crisp and fresh produce can make all the difference between a flavorful or a mediocre salad.

As well as buying good-quality ingredients, the storage and treatment of them is important. Always store salad vegetables in a cool, dark place, ideally in the vegetable compartment of your refrigerator. Direct sunlight and heat deteriorates the vitamin content of vegetables, as well as making them limp and unattractive.

Nuts are an important element of many of my recipes, because they partner salad vegetables so well and are also an excellent source of fiber. Due to their high oil content they do not have a good shelf life, so should be bought in small quantities, stored in an airtight container in a cool place, and used within a few weeks. To help bring out their flavor, they can be toasted before use, as described in the relevant recipes.

Another tip is to always dry washed salad leaves before dressing them. This keeps them crisp and makes it easier for the salad dressing to coat the leaves. For frequent salad-makers, a salad spinner is a worthwhile addition to your kitchen because it is the quickest and most effective way of drying leaves.

Preparing and eating food should not simply be a necessity for survival, but rather an enjoyable experience. Consequently, presentation of the food is important to create visual appeal. Salad ingredients, with their tantalizing variety of colors and textures, are the perfect medium for doing just this. Again freshness is vital for presenting appetizing and attractive salads. The vibrant photography in *Easy to Make Salads* captures the way in which a wide variety of different crisp leaves, combined with the red and orange of tomatoes, purple onions and the green and white hues of scallions, can provide limitless opportunities to provide a feast for the eyes and the appetite. Imagine yellow, green and orange bell peppers contrasting with the differing textures of black olives, roasted pecans, young asparagus spears, soft goat cheese and delicate quail eggs, all tossed lightly in glistening oils and aromatic herbs. To enhance the aesthetic appeal, leaves can be torn, herbs snipped, and vegetables attractively sliced. Those few extra moments spent arranging the salad can make all the difference.

Dressings, that other vital element of any good salad, should complement the tastes of the main ingredients and not dominate or disguise them. With all oil-and-vinegar dressings, the proportion of oil to vinegar is ultimately a matter of personal taste, but the classic ratio is one part vinegar to three parts oil.

Oils are used in virtually all salad dressings, and the most frequently used are olive oil, virgin olive oil, sunflower, grapeseed, hazelnut and walnut oils. It is generally accepted that some are more healthy than others – olive oil being a monosaturate is the ideal choice for cholesterol-watchers, while the nut oils, although not so healthy, are nonetheless delicious.

Most of the *Easy to Make Salads* have oil-based dressings, but do experiment with varying the suggested oils (and vinegars) to create your own version of a salad.

Oils do not have a long shelf life and, if kept for too long, will go rancid. Buy them in quantities appropriate to your needs. Likewise, avoid storing vinegars for long periods, as they become cloudy and very acidic.

Vinegar is a frequent partner of oil in salad dressings. White wine, red wine, tarragon, cider and balsamic vinegars are the most widely used, but there is also a large variety of other flavored vinegars, ranging from champagne, sherry and rice wine vinegar to store-bought ones with added herbs and spices.

It is easy to make this choice virtually infinite by flavoring both oils and vinegars yourself. For example, to make a spicy olive oil, add dried chilies, garlic cloves, black peppercorns and sprigs of rosemary to olive oil, or add chives, lemon peel and fennel seeds to sunflower oil, and fresh basil sprigs to extra virgin oil.

You can flavor your own vinegars too. Some examples are oregano and pink peppercorns in red wine vinegar, chervil and orange peel in champagne vinegar, mint sprigs in white wine vinegar, and sage and red onion slices in cider vinegar. These home-prepared flavored oils and vinegars should be kept in a sunny place for two weeks before use, to allow the flavors to develop. Fruit can also be used to sweeten vinegars:

STRAWBERRY OR RASPBERRY VINEGAR
Place 1 pound washed strawberries or raspberries in a large bowl and crush lightly. Pour over 2½ cups white wine vinegar. Cover the bowl with plastic wrap and leave for 4 days, stirring once a day. Strain liquid through cheesecloth into a saucepan, and add ½ cup superfine sugar. Heat gently until sugar has dissolved, then boil for 1 minute. Cool slightly, and pour fruit vinegar into sterilized bottles. Seal and leave to mature for 3 weeks. Fruit vinegars are best used within 6 months of preparation.

QUICK FRUIT VINAIGRETTE
Mango or Peach Vinaigrette is an unusual, but easy, dressing. It must be kept refrigerated and used within a few days of preparation. Place the flesh from 1 ripe, peeled mango or 1 large ripe peach in a food processor. Add 2 tablespoons white wine vinegar and 5 tablespoons grapeseed oil. Season with salt and pepper. Puree until the mixture is thick and smooth. These dressings are good served with cold meat and smoked chicken. Alternatively, add a tablespoon of chopped dill or cilantro, and serve them with smoked fish or cooked shrimp. Here are two classic recipes; both of which are good stand-bys to be used with any combination of leaves or vegetables of your choice.

CLASSIC VINAIGRETTE
Place 6 tablespoons olive oil, 2 tablespoons white wine vinegar or lemon juice, ½ teaspoon Dijon mustard, and sea salt and freshly ground black pepper in a screw-topped jar and shake well to combine. Refrigerate and use as required.

MAYONNAISE (makes 1¼ cups)
All the ingredients should be at room temperature to prevent the mayonnaise from curdling. Put 2 egg yolks, ½ teaspoon salt, 1 teaspoon Dijon mustard, freshly ground black pepper, and 1 tablespoon of wine vinegar in a food processor. Blend until well combined. With the motor running, gradually trickle in 1¼ cups olive oil, drop by drop to start with, then in a thin steady stream until all the oil has been added and you have smooth, thick mayonnaise. Add 1 more tablespoon of vinegar. Taste and adjust seasoning, and store in a sealed container in the refrigerator for up to 2 weeks. Lastly, salad making, like all cooking, should not be a chore! *Easy to Make Salads* is a collection of salads that are quick and easy to prepare, yet also creative and tasty. Some, such as *Cajun Shrimp Salad* and *Thai Beef Salad* have more involved preparation, but do not be put off trying them, because they, like all the recipes in this book, are described in easy steps, and the end result is well worth the effort.

Enjoy using this book, and may it inspire you to experiment and to create your own, individual salads. Happy Salad-making!

— 1 —
CLASSIC FAVORITES

INGREDIENTS

8 ounces green beans
8 ounces new potatoes
6½-ounce can tuna fish, drained
4 ripe tomatoes, quartered
4 hard-boiled eggs, quartered
8 anchovy fillets, halved and split lengthwise
1 tablespoon capers, rinsed and drained
2 crisp lettuce hearts, washed and separated into leaves
16 black olives
Dressing:
6 tablespoons extra virgin olive oil
2 tablespoons white wine vinegar
1 clove garlic, crushed
1 tablespoon Dijon mustard
½ teaspoon superfine sugar
1 tablespoon chopped fresh parsley
1 tablespoon chopped fresh basil

METHOD

Preparation time: 30 minutes

Top and tail the green beans, and cook them in boiling water for 1 minute. Drain and set aside. Slice the potatoes thickly, and cook in boiling, salted water until tender. Drain and let cool.

Whisk all the dressing ingredients together in a bowl until well combined. Season to taste. Flake the tuna into large chunks, and place in a bowl with the beans, potatoes, tomatoes, eggs, anchovies and capers. Add the dressing and toss together gently.

Line a serving bowl with the lettuce leaves and pile the tuna mixture into the center. Scatter the black olives over the top, and serve at room temperature with crusty bread.

Serves 4

INGREDIENTS

1 romaine lettuce
²⁄₃ cup virgin olive oil
2 thick slices white bread, crusts
    removed
4 anchovy fillets, drained, rinsed and
    dried
2 ounces Parmesan cheese
freshly ground black pepper
Dressing:
2 eggs
²⁄₃ cup virgin olive oil
juice of 1 lemon
½ teaspoon Worcestershire sauce
1 clove garlic, crushed
sea salt and freshly ground black
    pepper

METHOD

Preparation time: 30 minutes

Wash the lettuce leaves and dry them in a salad spinner. Tear the leaves into large pieces and place them in a salad bowl. Heat the olive oil in a skillet until moderately hot. Cut the bread into small cubes, and fry in the hot oil until crisp and golden. Remove with a slotted spoon and drain on paper towels. Chop the anchovies into tiny pieces.

Place the eggs in a pan of cold water, bring them to a boil, then reduce to a simmer and cook them for 2 minutes. Blend the remaining dressing ingredients together in a food processor until well combined. Break in the soft-boiled eggs and blend again until the dressing is creamy. Taste and adjust the seasoning, if necessary.

Just before serving, use a swivel peeler to flake the Parmesan cheese. Pour the dressing over the lettuce leaves and sprinkle with the cheese flakes and anchovy pieces. Scatter the croutons over the top, and grind some black pepper over the salad. Toss at the table and serve immediately.

NOTE:
The olive oil used to fry the croutons can be strained into a bottle when cool and used to fry other food.

Serves 4

INGREDIENTS

¾ cup walnut halves
6 stalks celery
4 red-skinned apples
1 tablespoon lemon juice
6 large radicchio leaves
Mayonnaise:
1 egg yolk
½ teaspoon Dijon mustard
¼ teaspoon salt
pinch of superfine sugar
freshly ground black pepper
⅔ cup grapeseed oil
1 tablespoon white wine vinegar

METHOD   Preparation time: 25 minutes

For the mayonnaise, place the egg yolk in a small bowl with the mustard, salt, sugar and pepper. Whisk together lightly until thoroughly combined. Start adding the oil drip by drip, whisking continuously until an emulsion is formed. When the mayonnaise begins to thicken, the oil may be added in a thin stream. Finally, blend in the vinegar, taste, and adjust the seasoning if necessary.

Preheat the oven to 375°F. Place the walnut halves on a baking sheet and bake them until they are toasted (about 10 minutes). Transfer to a plate and let cool. Wash the celery, remove any stringy fibers, and slice each stalk thinly. Quarter and core the apples, and cut them into neat chunks. Place the chunks in a small bowl and toss them in the lemon juice to prevent discoloration.

Wash and dry the radicchio leaves, and tear them in half. Use them to line a large salad bowl. Place the celery, drained apple chunks and toasted walnuts in a separate bowl. Pour the mayonnaise over, and toss well to combine. Spoon the mixture onto the salad leaves, and serve immediately.

NOTE:
If the mayonnaise curdles, gradually whisk in a tablespoon of hot water until the sauce is thick and shiny.

Serves 6–8

INGREDIENTS

7 ounces feta cheese
4 tomatoes
1 cucumber
1 small onion, thinly sliced
8 kalamata olives
8 large green olives
parsley and oregano sprigs to garnish
crusty sesame bread to serve
Dressing:
6 tablespoons virgin olive oil
2 tablespoons red wine vinegar
1 small clove garlic, crushed
1 tablespoon chopped fresh
  oregano
1 tablespoon chopped fresh parsley
sea salt and freshly ground black
  pepper
pinch of sugar

METHOD

Preparation time: 15 minutes

Place all the dressing ingredients in a bowl and whisk well to combine. Adjust the seasoning, if necessary, and set aside.

Cut the feta cheese into cubes, and place in a large salad bowl. Cut the tomatoes into wedges, and add these to the bowl. Quarter the cucumber and slice it into chunks. Add these to the bowl, along with the onions and olives.

Just before serving, pour the dressing over the salad and toss well to combine. Serve garnished with herb sprigs, and accompanied by warm sesame bread.

Serves 4

INGREDIENTS

1 large cucumber
1 teaspoon salt
½ lollo blondo loose-leaf lettuce,
   washed and separated into leaves
1 cup sliced, ripe strawberries
Dressing:
2 teaspoons pink peppercorns in
   brine
3 tablespoons sunflower oil
1 tablespoon balsamic vinegar
salt and freshly ground black pepper

METHOD   Preparation time: 25 minutes

Using a citrus stripper, remove strips of skin from the cucumber to create a ridged pattern. Slice it very thinly, then place on a plate and sprinkle with the salt. Let stand for 15 minutes to draw out excess moisture.

Drain the peppercorns on paper towels. Place them in a bowl, and crush coarsely with the back of a metal spoon. Add the oil and vinegar, and whisk the dressing together until well combined. Season to taste. Rinse the sliced cucumber and dry it thoroughly on paper towels.

To serve, arrange the lettuce on four individual plates. Garnish with alternating circles of cucumber and strawberries. Spoon some dressing over each portion, and serve immediately.

Serves 4

TOMATO AND ONION SALAD

INGREDIENTS

6 ounces orange cherry tomatoes
1 small purple onion
Dressing:
6 tablespoons extra virgin olive oil
2 tablespoons freshly squeezed lemon
  juice
salt and freshly ground black pepper
1 tablespoon chopped flat-leaf
  parsley

METHOD

Preparation time: 15 minutes

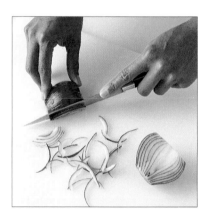

Wash and halve the cherry tomatoes and place them in a salad bowl. Peel the onion and cut into very thin strips, then add to the tomatoes.

Place all the dressing ingredients in a bowl and whisk well to combine. Season to taste.

About 10 minutes before serving, pour the dressing over the tomatoes and onions and mix well. Serve the salad at room temperature.

NOTE:
This salad can also be made with red cherry tomatoes if orange ones are unavailable.

Serves 4

INGREDIENTS

6 slices bacon
8 ounces hard French cheese, such
  as Comté or Cantal
4 tablespoons pine nuts
4 ounces butterhead lettuce
4 ounces oak leaf lettuce
Dressing:
1 teaspoon dark French mustard
¼ teaspoon salt
1 teaspoon superfine sugar
freshly ground black pepper
2 lightly beaten egg yolks
2 tablespoons cider vinegar
3 tablespoons chopped fresh parsley
  and thyme
4 tablespoons heavy cream

METHOD

Preparation time: 25 minutes

For the dressing, place the mustard, salt, sugar and pepper in a bowl. Gradually beat in the egg yolks and vinegar, whisking well until they are thoroughly combined. Place the bowl over a pan of simmering water and cook, stirring occasionally, until the mixture thickens (about 4–5 minutes). Stir in the chopped herbs and chill thoroughly. Fold in the cream just before serving.

Cook the slices of bacon under a hot broiler for about 5 minutes on each side, until they are crisp and golden. Let cool, and then snip the bacon into strips. Cut the cheese into small cubes. Dry-fry the pine nuts in a pan, turning them constantly to prevent them from burning. When they are golden, transfer to a plate and let cool. Separate the lettuces into leaves, and wash and dry them.

To serve, tear the lettuce leaves into bite-size pieces. Place them in a salad bowl, and scatter the bacon, cheese and pine nuts over the top. Spoon on a little of the cream dressing, and serve immediately, passing extra dressing separately.

Serves 4

INGREDIENTS

6 slices Canadian bacon
2 slices whole-wheat bread
1 large clove garlic, peeled
²/₃ cup olive oil
6 tomatoes
*½ small iceberg lettuce, finely
  shredded*
Dressing:
6 tablespoons olive oil
2 tablespoons sherry vinegar
2 tablespoons Blue Castello cheese
salt and freshly ground black pepper
pinch of paprika
pinch of sugar
2 tablespoons mayonnaise

METHOD

Preparation time: 25 minutes

Cook the bacon under a preheated broiler until it is crisp and golden (about 10–15 minutes). Set it aside to cool. Cut the bread into small cubes. Halve the clove of garlic, then crush the halves slightly to bruise them. Place the garlic in a pan with the olive oil, and heat the oil until it is moderately hot. Fry the bread cubes in batches until crisp, removing each batch with a slotted spoon and draining them on paper towels.

Wash the tomatoes and slice them into rings. Divide the shredded lettuce between four plates. Arrange the tomato slices over the lettuce. Using scissors, snip the bacon into small pieces and scatter them over the lettuce and tomato.

Place all the dressing ingredients, except the mayonnaise, in a food processor. Blend together until it is smooth and creamy. Add the mayonnaise, and blend together quickly. Taste and adjust the seasoning, if necessary. Spoon a quarter of the dressing over each salad, sprinkle some croutons over each portion, and serve immediately.

Serves 4

INGREDIENTS

8 ounces scamorze (smoked
  mozzarella cheese)
4 plum tomatoes
2 small avocados
2 teaspoons lemon juice
basil sprigs to garnish
warm ciabatta bread to serve
Vinaigrette:
6 tablespoons extra virgin olive oil
2 tablespoons red wine vinegar
6 large leaves of fresh basil
1 teaspoon Dijon mustard
2 tablespoons water
sea salt and freshly ground black
  pepper
pinch of sugar

METHOD

Preparation time: 15 minutes

Slice the scamorze as thinly as possible. Wash the tomatoes and cut them into several wedges. Peel, pit, and slice the avocados thinly. Place them on a plate, and sprinkle with lemon juice to prevent discoloration.

Place all the dressing ingredients in a food processor. Blend for a couple of minutes until well combined. Taste and adjust the seasoning, if necessary.

Divide the cheese, tomato wedges and sliced avocado between four plates. Drizzle the basil vinaigrette over the top, garnish each plate with a sprig of basil, and serve immediately with ciabatta bread.

NOTE:
If scamorze is unavailable, substitute smoked cheddar or Bavarian smoked cheese.

Serves 4

−2−
FRESH AND HEALTHY

STAR FRUIT, TOFU AND CHICORY SALAD

INGREDIENTS

8 ounces tofu (soybean curd)
1 tablespoon sesame oil
½ head chicory
1 large star fruit (carambola)
2 tablespoons toasted sunflower
  seeds
Dressing:
4 tablespoons sesame oil
3 tablespoons freshly squeezed
  orange juice
1 teaspoon clear honey
1 tablespoon white wine vinegar
salt and freshly ground black pepper

METHOD

Preparation time: 15 minutes

Cut the tofu into small cubes. Place the cubes on a baking sheet and sprinkle with the sesame oil. Cook under a preheated broiler for 5 minutes, turning the cubes over halfway through. Remove and set aside to cool.

Wash and dry the chicory, tear the leaves into bite-size pieces, and place in a salad bowl. Slice the star fruit thinly and add to the lettuce. Add the cooked tofu cubes to the bowl and set aside.

Place all the ingredients for the dressing in a screw-topped jar and shake well to combine. Taste and adjust the seasoning, if necessary. Just before serving, pour the dressing over the salad and toss lightly to combine. Sprinkle over the sunflower seeds, and serve immediately.

NOTE:
Smoked tofu can be used in this recipe to produce a stronger-tasting salad.

Serves 4

INGREDIENTS

2 cups low-fat cottage cheese
1 large red bell pepper
2 tablespoons snipped fresh chives
sea salt
1½ teaspoons tropical peppercorns
1 romaine lettuce
½ fresh pineapple
juice of 1 lime

METHOD

Preparation time: 20 minutes

Place the cottage cheese in a mixing bowl. Halve the bell pepper and remove the core. Cut the pepper into small diamond shapes and add to the cottage cheese. Stir in the chives and some salt. Crush the peppercorns with a mortar and pestle, and add to the cottage cheese. Mix well, taste, and adjust the seasoning if necessary.

Discard any damaged, outer leaves from the lettuce. Wash and dry the remaining leaves, and cut the larger leaves in half lengthwise. Peel the pineapple, quarter it, and remove the core. Cut each pineapple quarter lengthwise into four pieces.

Divide the lettuce leaves between four serving plates and add 2 pieces of pineapple to each plate. Place a quarter of the cottage cheese in a neat mound on each plate. Sprinkle a little lime juice over the lettuce leaves and pineapple, and serve immediately.

Serves 4

ASPARAGUS, SNOW PEA AND YELLOW PEPPER SALAD

INGREDIENTS

8 ounces asparagus, trimmed and
*   cut into 2-inch lengths*
6 ounces snow peas, strings removed
1 yellow bell pepper
Dressing:
4 tablespoons low-fat fromage blanc
freshly squeezed juice of 1 lemon
freshly squeezed juice of 1 lime
2 tablespoons snipped fresh chives
sea salt and freshly ground black
*   pepper*
lemon and lime zest to garnish

METHOD

Preparation time: 20 minutes

Blanch the asparagus in a pan of boiling, salted water for 2 minutes. Drain and refresh in cold water. Repeat the process with the snow peas, blanching them for 1 minute. Halve the bell pepper and remove the seeds. Slice the flesh into long strips.

Remove a little zest from the lemon and lime using a zester. Cover and set aside for the garnish. Whisk together the dressing ingredients in a small bowl until thoroughly combined. Adjust the seasoning if necessary.

Place the prepared vegetables in a salad bowl. Pour the dressing over and toss to combine. Sprinkle with the citrus zest, and serve immediately.

Serves 4

LETTUCE, RADISH AND GREEN BEAN SALAD

INGREDIENTS

7 ounces green beans
4 crisp lettuce hearts, each washed
  and cut into eight
12 radishes, washed and thinly sliced
1 tablespoon toasted sesame seeds
Dressing:
4 tablespoons sunflower oil
1 tablespoon sesame oil
1 tablespoon light tahini
2 tablespoons white wine vinegar
salt and freshly ground black pepper

METHOD

Preparation time: 15 minutes

Place all the dressing ingredients in a bowl and whisk together until well combined. Taste, adjust the seasoning if necessary, and set aside.

Top and tail the beans and cut them in half. Blanch them in a pan of boiling water for 2 minutes. Drain and refresh under cold water.

Place the lettuce, beans and radishes in a shallow serving bowl. Pour the dressing over, sprinkle with the toasted sesame seeds, and serve immediately.

Serves 4–6

GRAPEFRUIT, SHRIMP AND FETA CHEESE SALAD

INGREDIENTS

2 grapefruit
8 ounces cooked, peeled shrimp
2 cups cubed feta cheese
*1 head red Belgian endive, washed
  and separated into leaves*
*1 head yellow Belgian endive,
  washed and separated into leaves*
Dressing:
4 tablespoons light olive oil
2 tablespoons grapefruit juice
1 scallion, thinly sliced
1 tablespoon chopped fresh parsley
salt and freshly ground black pepper

METHOD   Preparation time: 15 minutes

Peel the grapefruit with a small sharp knife and divide the flesh into sections, cutting in between the membrane. Do this over a bowl to save the grapefruit juice for the dressing.

Place the dressing ingredients in a screw-topped jar and shake well to combine. Adjust the seasoning if necessary. (Discard any remaining grapefruit juice.) Arrange the endive leaves on a flat serving dish.

Place the shrimp, feta cheese and grapefruit sections in a salad bowl. Pour the dressing over and toss lightly to combine. Spoon this mixture over the endive leaves, and serve immediately.

Serves 4

INGREDIENTS

½ cup skinless hazelnuts
8 ounces mixed salad leaves, such as
  chicory, lollo rosso, oak leaf,
  romaine, arugula, radicchio and
  corn salad
Dressing:
4 tablespoons hazelnut oil
1 tablespoon sunflower oil
4 teaspoons raspberry vinegar
salt and freshly ground black pepper
pinch of sugar

METHOD

Preparation time: 20 minutes

Preheat the oven to 375°F. Place the hazelnuts on a baking sheet and cook them until they are pale golden (about 10 minutes). Transfer them to a plate and let cool.

Tear the larger salad leaves into bite-size pieces and keep the small ones whole. Wash the leaves and dry them in a salad spinner or between clean dish towels. Transfer to a serving bowl.

Halve the toasted hazelnuts and add these to the bowl. Place the dressing ingredients in a screw-topped jar and shake thoroughly to combine. Taste and adjust the seasoning if necessary, and pour the dressing over the salad leaves. Toss lightly to combine, and serve immediately.

NOTE:
Try using walnuts and walnut oil instead of hazelnuts and hazelnut oil to vary the flavor of this salad.

Serves 4

CARROT, CELERY, APPLE AND BRAZIL NUT SALAD

INGREDIENTS

6 ounces carrots
6 ounces celery
1 large eating apple
2 teaspoons lemon juice
½ cup brazil nuts
Dressing:
6 tablespoons grapeseed oil
2 tablespoons cider vinegar
3 tablespoons chopped mixed herbs,
    such as parsley, chives, chervil and
    mint
salt and freshly ground black pepper

METHOD

Preparation time: 20 minutes

Cut the carrots into julienne strips. Wash the celery and slice it thinly on the diagonal. Cut the apple into quarters, core it, and slice it very thinly. Sprinkle the lemon juice over the apple slices to prevent discoloration.

Place all the dressing ingredients in a screw-topped jar and shake well to combine thoroughly. Season to taste.

Place the carrots, celery, apple and brazil nuts in a large bowl. Pour the dressing over the top. Toss to combine, and serve immediately.

Serves 4

INGREDIENTS

1 ripe honeydew melon
2 pears
2 teaspoons lime juice
½ curly endive, washed and torn into
  small pieces
½ cup corn salad, washed
*julienne strips of lime and mint sprigs
  to garnish*
Dressing:
6 tablespoons grapeseed oil
3 tablespoons freshly squeezed lime
  juice
pinch of sea salt
½ teaspoon crushed dried green
  peppercorns
1 tablespoon chopped fresh mint

METHOD

Preparation time: 25 minutes

Halve the melon and scoop out the seeds. Using a melon baller, scoop out the flesh into a bowl. Peel, core, and thinly slice the pears. Sprinkle with lime juice to prevent discoloration.

Place the dressing ingredients in a screw-topped jar and shake well to combine. Adjust the seasoning if necessary, and set aside.

Place the curly endive and the corn salad on a large platter. Arrange the fruit on top and drizzle the dressing over. Serve immediately, garnished with the lime julienne strips and mint sprigs.

Serves 4

FENNEL, SUGAR SNAP AND CUCUMBER SALAD

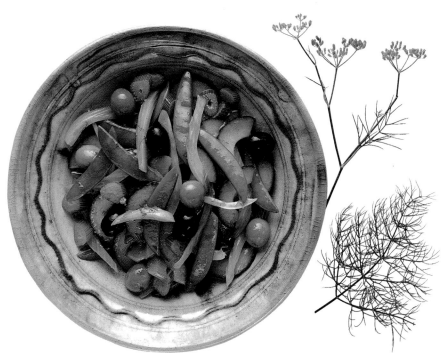

INGREDIENTS

1 large head Florence fennel
1 tablespoon lemon juice
4 ounces sugar snap peas, strings
  removed
1 cucumber
12 black olives
12 green olives
Dressing:
6 tablespoons olive oil
2 tablespoons white wine vinegar
1 tablespoon dark French mustard
1 clove garlic, crushed
sea salt and freshly ground black
  pepper
pinch of sugar

METHOD

Preparation time: 15 minutes

Remove the feathery fennel tops, chop them finely, and add to the dressing ingredients in a small bowl. Whisk everything together to combine. Adjust the seasoning if necessary, and set aside.

Slice the fennel thinly, then blanch it in boiling water with the lemon juice for 2 minutes. Drain and refresh under cold water. Blanch the sugar snap peas for 1 minute. Drain and refresh. Halve the cucumber lengthwise, remove the seeds with a teaspoon, and slice thickly.

Place the prepared vegetables and olives in a salad bowl. Pour the dressing over the top, toss well, and serve immediately.

Serves 4

26

SUMMER HERB AND FLOWER SALAD

INGREDIENTS

*3 ounces mixed herbs and salad
  leaves per person, from the
  following suggestions: flat-leaf
  parsley, chervil, basil, chives and
  flowers, nasturtium leaves and
  flowers, sage and flowers, borage
  flowers, marigold flowers, edible
  pansy, violet flowers, arugula,
  sorrel, corn salad, lovage, curly
  endive, baby spinach leaves*
Dressing:
3 ounces watercress
1 clove garlic
1 tablespoon chopped shallot
2 tablespoons rice wine vinegar
5 tablespoons olive oil
salt and freshly ground black pepper

METHOD

Preparation time: 20 minutes

Wash the leaves and dry them
between clean dish towels, taking
care not to bruise them too much.
Tear the leaves up into bite-size
pieces and place them in a salad
bowl. Sprinkle any flowers you are
using over the top, and set the salad
aside.

Wash the watercress and remove any
thick stalks or roots. Place it in a food
processor with the garlic, shallots,
vinegar, oil, salt and pepper, and
blend in short bursts until everything
is thoroughly combined and the
dressing is smooth. Taste and adjust
the seasoning if necessary.

Pour the dressing into a small bowl
and serve the salad leaves separately,
allowing people to dress their salads
individually.

NOTE:
Fresh herbs will last for a few days if
they are kept in well-sealed plastic
bags in the refrigerator.

Serves 4–6

27

Red Lettuce and Mushroom Salad

INGREDIENTS

½ radicchio lettuce
½ lollo rosso, loose-leaf lettuce
½ oak leaf lettuce
6 ounces button mushrooms
¾ cup pecans
Dressing:
5 tablespoons light olive oil
3 tablespoons freshly squeezed lemon
 juice
3 tablespoons plain yogurt
4 teaspoons chopped fresh thyme
1 teaspoon clear honey
salt and freshly ground black pepper

METHOD

Preparation time: 25 minutes

Separate the lettuce leaves and break any large leaves into bite-size pieces. Wash the pieces and dry them using a salad spinner or clean, dry dish towels. Place them in a large bowl and set aside.

Wipe the mushrooms clean and quarter them. Add them to the bowl of lettuce. Spread the pecans out on a baking sheet and toast them under a moderately hot broiler for 5 minutes, turning them occasionally to prevent them from burning. Let cool while preparing the dressing.

Place all the dressing ingredients in a small bowl and whisk together until thoroughly combined. Taste and adjust the seasoning if necessary. Add the cooled pecans to the lettuce and mushrooms, pour the dressing over, toss well, and serve immediately.

Serves 6

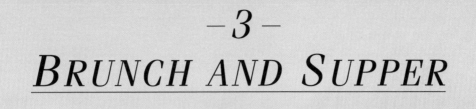

— 3 —
BRUNCH AND SUPPER

INGREDIENTS

2 red bell peppers, halved and cored
2 orange bell peppers, halved and
cored
2 cups crumbled Dolcelatte cheese
8 ounces fresh arugula, washed
ciabatta bread to serve
Dressing:
2-3 tablespoons white wine vinegar
6 tablespoons extra virgin olive oil
1 clove garlic, crushed
1 teaspoon superfine sugar
1 tablespoon Dijon mustard
2 tablespoons snipped fresh chives
salt and freshly ground black pepper

METHOD

Preparation time: 20 minutes

Place the bell peppers, skin side up, under a hot broiler and cook for 8–10 minutes until the skins begin to blacken. Remove them and cover with damp paper towels (this helps to loosen the skins, making them easier to peel). When cool enough to handle, peel the peppers and cut into neat strips.

Prepare the dressing by shaking all the ingredients together in a screw-topped jar. Season to taste.

To serve, place the arugula in a shallow salad bowl, top with the pepper strips and crumbled cheese. Pour the dressing over, toss well, and serve immediately with hot ciabatta bread.

Serves 4

BRESAOLA AND HEARTS OF PALM SALAD

INGREDIENTS

14-ounce can hearts of palm
1 small head Belgian endive
½ lollo rosso, loose-leaf lettuce
2 tablespoons pine nuts
12 thin slices Bresaola
Dressing:
6 tablespoons extra virgin olive oil
1½ tablespoons balsamic vinegar
1½ teaspoons Dijon mustard
2 teaspoons chopped fresh sage
salt and freshly ground black pepper
1 tablespoon water

METHOD

Preparation time: 20 minutes

Drain the hearts of palm and cut each piece into thick slices, on the diagonal. Divide the endive into leaves, and wash and dry it. Wash and dry the lollo rosso, and break the leaves into large pieces.

Place all the dressing ingredients in a small bowl and whisk together until thoroughly combined. Taste and adjust the seasoning if necessary. Place the pine nuts on a baking sheet and cook under a preheated broiler for about 4 minutes, turning occasionally until they are toasted. Set aside to cool.

To serve, divide the salad leaves between four plates. Place three slices of Bresaola on each plate and divide the hearts of palm between the four plates. Sprinkle the pine nuts over the top. Spoon some dressing over each portion, and serve immediately.

NOTE:
Bresaola is cured beef. Italian salami could be substituted.

Serves 4

AVOCADO, LABNA BALL AND CHERRY TOMATO SALAD

INGREDIENTS

1 pound cherry tomatoes
15 labna balls in oil
2 avocados
1 batavia or escarole lettuce
Dressing:
6 tablespoons extra virgin olive oil
2 tablespoons white wine vinegar
1 teaspoon finely chopped shallot
½ teaspoon Dijon mustard
*sea salt and freshly ground black
  pepper*

METHOD

Preparation time: 25 minutes

Place all the dressing ingredients in a screw-topped jar and shake well to combine. Taste and adjust the seasoning if necessary, and set the dressing aside to allow the flavors to develop.

Wash and halve the cherry tomatoes. Drain the labna balls and halve them carefully, taking care not to break them up too much. Peel the avocados, remove the pits, and slice the flesh thinly. Remove and discard any damaged outer leaves from the lettuce, wash and dry the remaining leaves, and tear them into bite-size pieces.

To serve, place the lettuce in a large salad bowl. Put the tomatoes, labna balls and avocado slices in a mixing bowl. Pour the dressing over and toss gently. Spoon this mixture on top of the lettuce leaves, grind over some black pepper, and serve immediately.

NOTE:
Labna balls are Greek-style strained yogurt balls and are available in Greek or Turkish delicatessens. If they are unavailable, try using individual mozzarella cheese balls.

Serves 6

LEEK AND QUAIL EGG SALAD

INGREDIENTS

1 pound young leeks
16 quail eggs
1 bunch watercress
20 kalamata olives
Vinaigrette:
6 tablespoons light olive oil
1½ tablespoons balsamic vinegar
2 tablespoons chopped flat-leaf
   parsley
sea salt and freshly ground black
   pepper

METHOD

Preparation time: 30 minutes

Wash and trim the leeks and slice them fairly thinly, on the diagonal. Cook them in boiling, salted water for 3–4 minutes until just tender. Drain and refresh them under cold water, and set aside.

Place the quail eggs in a pan of cold water and bring them to a boil. Reduce the heat to a simmer and cook the eggs for 3 minutes. Plunge them into cold water and, when they are cool enough to handle, peel them. Trim the tough stalks from the watercress, and wash and dry the leaves.

Place the vinaigrette ingredients in a screw-topped jar and shake well to combine. Taste and adjust the seasoning if necessary. To serve, divide the watercress between four plates. Place the leeks and olives in a bowl and pour the dressing over, toss to combine, and divide the mixture between the four plates. Halve 8 of the eggs and place 2 whole eggs and 4 halves on each plate. Serve immediately.

Serves 4

INGREDIENTS

8 ounces mixed radicchio lettuce and
  corn salad
generous handful of Italian flat-leaf
  parsley leaves
8 slices French bread
2 tablespoons extra virgin olive oil
8 ounces soft goat cheese
freshly ground black pepper
Dressing:
6 tablespoons virgin olive oil
2 tablespoons white wine vinegar
2 tablespoons dark French mustard
3 cloves garlic, crushed
¼ teaspoon superfine sugar
salt and freshly ground black pepper

METHOD

Preparation time: 20 minutes

Whisk the dressing ingredients together until thoroughly combined. Taste and adjust the seasoning, if necessary, and set aside. Tear the radicchio leaves into bite-size pieces. Wash the salad and parsley leaves, and dry them in a salad spinner. Transfer to a mixing bowl and set aside.

Brush one side of each piece of bread lightly with olive oil and toast them under a moderately hot broiler until lightly golden. Remove from the broiler, and slice or spread the goat cheese onto the untoasted sides of the bread. Grind over some black pepper and cook under a moderate broiler for a few more minutes, until the cheese melts.

To serve, pour the dressing over the salad leaves and toss well. Divide the salad between four plates. Top each plate with 2 slices of freshly broiled goat cheese bread, and serve immediately.

Serves 4

WARM MUSHROOM AND PECORINO SALAD

INGREDIENTS

12 ounces mixed mushrooms, such
   as brown, oyster, shiitake,
   chanterelles, cèpes, field and girolle
6 tablespoons extra virgin olive oil
2 ounces arugula
4 ounces Pecorino cheese
1 tablespoon lemon juice
sea salt and freshly ground black
   pepper
crusty bread to serve

METHOD

Preparation time: 20 minutes

Wipe the mushrooms and slice any large ones. Heat 2 tablespoons of the oil in a large skillet and sauté half the mushrooms for 1 minute, stirring constantly. Season them with salt and pepper, and transfer them to a bowl. Cook the remaining mushrooms in the same way with 2 more tablespoons of the oil.

Wash and dry the arugula, and place it in a shallow serving bowl. Use a swivel peeler and slice the Pecorino cheese into thin slivers. Set it aside.

Whisk together the remaining olive oil and the lemon juice with some salt and pepper, and drizzle this over the arugula. Spoon the sautéed mushrooms into the center, sprinkle the Pecorino cheese over the top, and serve immediately with warm crusty bread.

Serves 4

INGREDIENTS

6 ounces mixed salad leaves
4 ripe figs
8 artichoke hearts in oil, drained
4 tablespoons virgin olive oil
1 tablespoon balsamic vinegar
sea salt and freshly ground black
  pepper
8 large slices prosciutto

METHOD   **Preparation time:** 20 minutes

Tear the larger salad leaves into bite-size pieces. Wash and dry them using a salad spinner or clean dish towels. Set them aside.

Peel the skin off the figs using a small sharp knife. Cut each fig into quarters, cutting almost through to the base so each fig remains intact. Halve the artichoke hearts. Place 3 tablespoons of the olive oil and the balsamic vinegar in a screw-topped jar and shake well to combine. Season lightly with salt and pepper. Set aside.

To serve, toss the lettuce leaves lightly in the dressing and divide them between four plates. Place 2 slices of ham, 1 fig, and 4 artichoke halves on each plate. Drizzle the remaining tablespoon of olive oil lightly over each portion. Grind over some black pepper, and serve immediately.

Serves 4

WARM CHICKEN LIVER, SAGE AND ORANGE SALAD

INGREDIENTS

*8 ounces mixed green salad leaves,
  such as lollo blondo loose-leaf,
  chicory and escarole lettuces
2 large oranges
1 pound chicken livers
salt and freshly ground black pepper
¼ cup unsalted butter
2 tablespoons chopped fresh sage
Dressing:
4 tablespoons sunflower oil
2 tablespoons reserved orange juice
1 teaspoon grated orange zest
1 teaspoon Dijon mustard
sea salt and freshly ground black
  pepper*

METHOD

Preparation time: 25 minutes

Tear the lettuce leaves into bite-size pieces, and wash and dry them. Place them in a shallow serving bowl and set aside. Grate 1 teaspoon of orange zest for the dressing; then peel the oranges and, using a small sharp knife, cut in between the membranes to divide the flesh into sections. Do this over a bowl to collect the orange juice for the dressing.

Trim and slice the livers. Rinse them and pat them dry on paper towels. Season well with salt and pepper. Melt the butter in a large skillet and, when it begins to foam, add the livers and chopped sage. Cook over a medium heat, stirring occasionally until the livers are just cooked through (about 5 minutes).

Place the dressing ingredients in a screw-topped jar and shake well to combine. Taste and adjust the seasoning if necessary. To serve, spoon the warm chicken livers and the orange sections over the lettuce leaves, pour the dressing over, and serve immediately.

Serves 4

INGREDIENTS

12 ounces smoked chicken
5 halves of sun-dried tomatoes in oil
3 stalks celery
16 green olives
½ batavia or escarole lettuce
Dressing:
2 tablespoons sunflower oil
2 tablespoons olive oil
1 teaspoon grainy mustard
1 tablespoon red wine vinegar
1 clove garlic, crushed
sea salt and freshly ground black
  pepper
pinch of sugar

METHOD

Preparation time: 25 minutes

Remove the skin from the smoked chicken and cut the flesh into neat, bite-size pieces. Slice the sun-dried tomatoes into thin strips. Wash the celery and slice thinly on the diagonal.

Put all the dressing ingredients in a small bowl and whisk them together until thoroughly combined. Taste and adjust the seasoning if necessary. Separate the lettuce into leaves, and wash and dry them.

To serve, line a shallow bowl with the lettuce leaves. Place the chicken, sun-dried tomatoes, celery and green olives in a mixing bowl. Pour the dressing over and toss well to combine. Spoon the chicken mixture into the center of the salad leaves, and serve immediately.

Serves 4

INGREDIENTS

20 baby new potatoes
6 ounces smoked salmon (lox)
2 crisp lettuce hearts
1 tablespoon capers
Dressing:
3 tablespoons cream cheese
1½ tablespoons lemon juice
6 tablespoons sunflower oil
4 teaspoons snipped fresh chives
sea salt and freshly ground black
  pepper
pinch of sugar

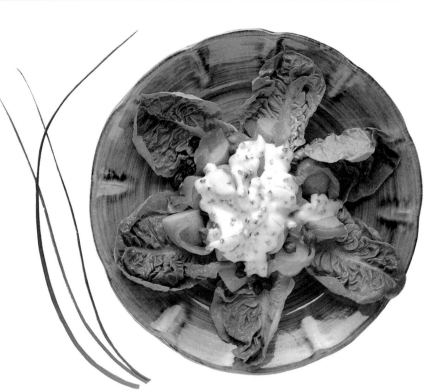

METHOD

Preparation time: 25 minutes

Scrub the potatoes and halve them. Bring a pan of salted water to a boil, and cook the potatoes until they are tender (about 8–10 minutes). Drain, refresh them under cold water, and set aside. Slice the salmon into thin strips and set it aside.

Place all the dressing ingredients, except the chives, in a food processor and blend until well combined. Add the chives and blend again for a few seconds. Taste and adjust the seasoning if necessary.

Separate the lettuce leaves, wash and dry them, and then use them to line a shallow bowl. Pile the potatoes and salmon into the center. Sprinkle the capers on top and pour the dressing over. Serve immediately.

Serves 4

PEAR, STILTON AND WALNUT SALAD

INGREDIENTS

6 ounces Stilton cheese
1 tablespoon walnut oil
½ cup walnut pieces
pinch of sea salt
12 large radicchio leaves
3 small pears, quartered and cored
2 tablespoons lemon juice
Dressing:
1 tablespoon walnut oil
2 tablespoons sunflower oil
1 tablespoon red wine vinegar
sea salt and freshly ground black
  pepper
¼ teaspoon superfine sugar

METHOD

Preparation time: 25 minutes

Remove the rind from the Stilton and crumble the cheese into small cubes. Heat the walnut oil in a small pan and cook the walnut pieces over a medium heat for 2-3 minutes. Remove with a slotted spoon, drain on paper towels, and sprinkle with sea salt. Wash and dry the radicchio leaves.

Slice the pears thinly and toss them in a shallow bowl with the lemon juice to prevent them discoloring. Place the ingredients for the dressing in a small bowl and whisk together until thoroughly combined. Taste and adjust the seasoning if necessary.

To serve, tear the lettuce leaves into quarters and divide them between four plates. Drain the lemon juice from the pears, and add the Stilton and walnuts to the bowl. Pour the dressing over and toss well to combine. Divide the pear, cheese and nut mixture between the four plates, and serve immediately.

Serves 4

SPINACH, EGG AND SMOKED HAM SALAD

INGREDIENTS

8 ounces baby spinach leaves
6 thick slices smoked ham
4 eggs
3 slices white bread, crusts removed
olive oil for frying
Vinaigrette:
4 tablespoons olive oil
1 tablespoon cider vinegar
1 tablespoon mayonnaise
1 teaspoon grainy mustard
1 large clove garlic, crushed
salt and freshly ground black pepper

METHOD

Preparation time: 25 minutes

Wash and dry the spinach leaves and place them in a large bowl. Slice the ham into thin strips and add to the spinach. Place the eggs in a pan of cold water, bring the water to a boil, and boil the eggs for 7–8 minutes to hard-boil them. Run under cold water until they are cool enough to handle, then peel off the shells.

Cut the bread into ½-inch squares. Pour enough olive oil into a pan to fill it to a depth of ½ inch, heat, and then fry the bread in batches until golden. Drain the croutons on paper towels to remove excess oil.

Place the dressing ingredients in a screw-topped jar and shake well to combine. Taste and adjust the seasoning if necessary. To serve, pour the dressing over the spinach and ham, toss gently to combine, and divide the salad between four plates. Quarter the eggs and place an egg on each plate. Divide the croutons between the plates, and serve immediately.

Serves 4

TUNA AND TOMATO SALAD CUPS

INGREDIENTS

4 ripe beefsteak tomatoes
6½-ounce can tuna chunks in water
1 cucumber, cut into small cubes
12 pitted black olives, sliced
2 tablespoons snipped fresh chives
½ cup plain yogurt
salt and freshly ground black pepper
½ iceberg lettuce
3 tablespoons light olive oil
1 tablespoon lemon juice
rye bread to serve

METHOD

Preparation time: 30 minutes

Slice the tops off the tomatoes and reserve them. Using a teaspoon, scoop out the seeds and flesh from the tomatoes and discard. Sprinkle a little salt into each tomato shell, and turn upside down on paper towels to drain while preparing the other ingredients.

Drain the tuna and flake it into small chunks. Place it in a mixing bowl with the cucumber, olives, chives and yogurt. Season the mixture well with salt and pepper, and toss gently until everything is well-coated in yogurt. Taste and adjust the seasoning if necessary.

Shred the lettuce and place it in a mixing bowl. Whisk together the oil, lemon juice and some salt and pepper, and pour this over the lettuce. Toss lightly to combine and divide the lettuce between four serving plates. Spoon a quarter of the tuna mixture into each tomato, replace the lids at an angle, and place a tomato on each plate of lettuce. Serve immediately with rye bread.

Serves 4

– 4 –
GRAINS, BEANS AND PASTA

WHEAT BERRY SALAD WITH SUNFLOWER SEEDS

INGREDIENTS

2 cups wheat berries
4 tablespoons sunflower seeds
1 bunch scallions
2 bunches watercress
3 tablespoons chopped fresh basil
3 tablespoons chopped fresh dill
Dressing:
6 tablespoons grapeseed oil
2 tablespoons balsamic vinegar
1 tablespoon grainy mustard
*sea salt and freshly ground black
  pepper*

METHOD   Preparation time: 15 minutes

Soak the wheat berries in cold water overnight. Place the wheat berries in a pan of fresh water, bring to a boil, and simmer for about 1 hour until they are tender but still retain a chewy texture. Some of the berries will pop open to reveal the white grain inside.

Place the sunflower seeds in a skillet and dry-fry them for a couple of minutes, turning frequently to prevent them from burning. Set them aside to cool. Wash and trim the scallions, and slice them thinly. Place the dressing ingredients in a screw-topped jar and shake well to combine. Taste and adjust the seasoning if necessary, and set it aside.

Discard any tough stalks from the watercress, and wash and dry it. Use it to line a shallow serving bowl. Place the wheat berries, sunflower seeds, scallions and chopped herbs in a mixing bowl. Pour the dressing over and toss well to combine. Taste and adjust the seasoning if necessary. Spoon this mixture onto the bed of watercress, and serve immediately.

Serves 6

44

INGREDIENTS

¼ cup wild rice
¾ cup long-grain rice
2 skinned, boned chicken breasts
2 tablespoons peanut oil
6 ounces green beans
1 red bell pepper
*4 tablespoons coarsely chopped
  tarragon*
½ cup salted cashews
Dressing:
*½ teaspoon green peppercorns in
  brine*
6 tablespoons peanut oil
2 tablespoons tarragon vinegar
2 teaspoons Dijon mustard
*sea salt and freshly ground black
  pepper*
pinch of sugar

METHOD

Preparation time: 30 minutes

Cook the wild rice in boiling, salted water for 30–35 minutes until it is tender. Drain and refresh it under cold water, and set it aside. Cook the long-grain rice in boiling, salted water for 8–10 minutes until cooked. Drain and refresh it, then set aside.

Slice the chicken into strips and season it well. Fry it with the peanut oil for 4–5 minutes until golden and cooked through. Set it aside to cool. Top and tail the beans and cut them into 1-inch pieces. Cook them in boiling, salted water for 2 minutes. Drain and refresh them. Halve the bell pepper, remove the core and seeds, and chop the pepper into large dice. Place all the prepared ingredients in a bowl, and add the tarragon and cashews.

Chop the peppercorns finely and place all the dressing ingredients in a screw-topped jar. Shake well to combine. Pour the dressing over the salad ingredients and toss well. Taste and adjust the seasoning if necessary, and serve immediately.

Serves 6

INGREDIENTS

2 cups canned red kidney beans
2 cups canned black-eyed peas
1 cup canned white lima beans
3 stalks celery
5 scallions
Dressing:
6 tablespoons sunolive oil
1½ tablespoons white wine vinegar
4 tablespoons chopped fresh cilantro
salt and freshly ground black pepper

METHOD
Preparation time: 15 minutes

Rinse the beans under cold running water, and then set them aside in a colander to drain. Wash the celery and remove any stringy fibers with a small, sharp knife. Cut the celery on the diagonal into ¼-inch slices.

Wash and dry the scallions, and cut both the white and green parts into ¼-inch slices. Place all the dressing ingredients in a small bowl and whisk together to form an emulsion. Taste and adjust the seasoning if necessary.

Place the beans, celery and scallions in a large salad bowl. Pour the dressing over and toss to combine thoroughly. If time permits, let the salad stand for about an hour before serving to allow the flavors to develop.

Serves 6

BORLOTTI BEAN, AVOCADO AND GRUYÈRE SALAD

INGREDIENTS

4 cups canned borlotti (saligia) beans
4 ounces Gruyère cheese
1 large or 2 small avocados
1 tablespoon lemon juice
Dressing:
6 tablespoons rapeseed oil
2½ tablespoons white wine vinegar
2 teaspoons Dijon mustard
1 egg yolk
¼ teaspoon paprika
sea salt and freshly ground black
    pepper
pinch of sugar

METHOD

Preparation time: 20 minutes

Place the borlotti beans in a colander and rinse them thoroughly under cold water. Drain and transfer them to a large salad bowl. Grate the cheese and add to the bowl of beans.

Peel and halve the avocado, remove the pit, and dice the flesh into neat chunks. Toss the chunks with the lemon juice in a small bowl to prevent discoloration. Place all the dressing ingredients in a food processor and blend until thoroughly combined and a smooth dressing is produced. Taste and adjust the seasoning, adding more paprika if it is not spicy enough.

To serve, drain the avocado chunks and add them to the bowl of beans and cheese. Season well with salt and pepper. Pour the creamy paprika dressing over, toss gently to combine, and serve immediately.

Serves 6–8

INGREDIENTS

8 ounces dried penne pasta
2 eggs
½ cup extra virgin olive oil
3 cloves garlic
4 shallots
1 large red chili
4 tablespoons chopped fresh cilantro
2 tablespoons capers
1 tablespoon white wine vinegar
sea salt and freshly ground black
  pepper
8 black olives
8 green olives

METHOD   Preparation time: 30 minutes

Place a few drops of oil in a pan of boiling, salted water, and cook the penne for about 10 minutes. Drain and refresh under cold water, then set aside. Cook the eggs in a pan of boiling water for 10 minutes to hard-boil them. Drain and plunge them into cold water until they are cool enough to handle, then peel them.

Peel the garlic and slice it into thin slivers. Peel the shallots and slice them thinly. Seed and slice the chili. Heat 2 tablespoons of the oil in a skillet and cook the garlic, shallots and chili for 5-6 minutes until crisp and golden. Remove with a slotted spoon and drain on paper towels.

Place the remaining oil, chopped cilantro, capers, vinegar and seasoning in a screw-topped jar and shake well until thoroughly combined. To serve, place the pasta and olives in a salad bowl. Pour the dressing over and toss well to combine. Quarter the eggs and arrange them on top of the salad. Sprinkle with the fried shallot mixture, and serve immediately.

Serves 4

ROQUEFORT AND PASTA SALAD

INGREDIENTS

1 tablespoon vegetable oil
6 slices bacon
1 red bell pepper
6 ounces pasta shapes
1½ cups cubed Roquefort cheese
Vinaigrette:
6 tablespoons olive oil
2 tablespoons red wine vinegar
1 clove garlic, crushed
2 tablespoons snipped chives
1 teaspoon Dijon mustard
salt and freshly ground black pepper

METHOD

Preparation time: 30 minutes

Heat the oil in a large skillet and cook the bacon slices, turning them once, until they are golden (about 5 minutes). When they are cool enough to handle, cut them into thick strips using scissors.

Halve the bell pepper, and remove the seeds and core. Slice the pepper into long, thin strips. Place the vinaigrette ingredients in a screw-topped jar and shake well until thoroughly combined. Taste and adjust the seasoning if necessary.

Cook the pasta for 8–10 minutes in a pan of boiling, salted water, to which a few drops of oil have been added. (This will prevent the pasta from sticking.) When cooked al dente, drain the pasta and transfer to a large salad bowl. Add the bacon, cheese and pepper to the bowl, pour the dressing over, and toss to combine. Serve immediately while the pasta is still warm.

Serves 4–6

ORECCHIETTE, BROCCOLI AND PINE NUT SALAD

INGREDIENTS

6 ounces orecchiette pasta
1 pound broccoli
4 tablespoons pine nuts
Dressing:
6 tomatoes
3 anchovy fillets, finely chopped
4 tablespoons white wine vinegar
6 tablespoons virgin olive oil
freshly ground black pepper

METHOD

Preparation time: 30 minutes

Cook the pasta for 10 minutes in a pan of boiling, salted water, to which a few drops of oil have been added to prevent the pasta from sticking. Drain and refresh the pasta under cold water, and set it aside. Divide the broccoli into florets, and cook in a pan of boiling, salted water for 3–4 minutes. Drain and refresh under cold water.

Place the pine nuts on a baking sheet and cook them under a hot broiler for a few minutes until golden, turning them frequently to prevent burning. Set them aside to cool. Peel and seed the tomatoes, and place them in a food processor with the remaining dressing ingredients. Blend to a thick, smooth dressing. Taste and adjust the seasoning if necessary.

Place the pasta, broccoli and pine nuts in a salad bowl. Pour the dressing over and toss well. If time permits, refrigerate the salad for about an hour to allow the flavors to develop.

NOTE:
To remove tomato skins easily, cut a cross at the base of each tomato, place them in a bowl, and cover with boiling water. When the skins begin to "pop," remove the tomatoes from the water, cool, and peel.

Serves 4–6

INGREDIENTS

1 pound frozen fava beans
12 dried apricots
½ cup blanched almonds
2 orange bell peppers
12 slices Italian salami
Dressing:
6 tablespoons virgin olive oil
2 tablespoons cider vinegar
2 teaspoons grainy mustard
sea salt and freshly ground black
  pepper
pinch of sugar

METHOD

Preparation time: 25 minutes

Cook the fava beans in a pan of boiling, salted water until they are tender (about 5–6 minutes). Drain and refresh them under cold water. Slice the apricots into thin strips and place them in a large salad bowl with the drained beans.

Place the almonds on a baking sheet, and toast them under a hot broiler for 3–4 minutes until they are golden. Let cool, then add them to the bowl. Halve and core the bell peppers, and chop them into large dice. Chop the salami into long strips. Add the peppers and salami to the bowl.

Place the ingredients for the dressing in a small bowl and whisk them together until thoroughly combined. Taste and adjust the seasoning if necessary. Pour the dressing over the salad ingredients and toss well to combine. If time permits, let the salad stand for an hour before serving to allow the flavors to develop.

Serves 6

COUSCOUS AND MEDITERRANEAN VEGETABLE SALAD

INGREDIENTS

1⅓ cups couscous
1 medium eggplant, about 8 ounces
4 ounces zucchini
1 orange bell pepper
1 yellow bell pepper
2 tablespoons olive oil
2 tablespoons pine nuts
1 purple onion
2 tablespoons raisins
Dressing:
2 teaspoons lime zest
1 tablespoon fresh lime juice
2 tablespoons chopped flat-leaf
  parsley
1 clove garlic
3 tablespoons virgin olive oil
sea salt
pinch of sugar
¼-½ teaspoon harissa paste

METHOD

Preparation time: 30 minutes

Place the couscous in a bowl and just cover with boiling water. Let stand for about 10 minutes to allow the grains to swell. When all the water has been absorbed, separate the grains, using your fingers, and set aside.

Halve the eggplant, zucchini and bell peppers lengthwise, remove the cores from the peppers, and use 1 tablespoon of the oil to brush the vegetables all over. Lay them skin-side up on a broiler rack, and cook until the skins are charred and the vegetables are cooked (about 10 minutes on each side).

Cool the broiled vegetables, remove the skins from the peppers, then dice all the vegetables into neat chunks and set aside.

Peel the onion and chop it finely. Place the remaining tablespoon of olive oil in a small pan, and cook the pine nuts for about 1 minute until they are golden. Remove with a slotted spoon and drain on paper towels.

Grate 2 teaspoons of lime zest and then squeeze the juice from the lime. Crush the garlic. Place all the dressing ingredients in a screw-topped jar and shake well to combine. Taste and adjust the seasoning and the amount of harissa paste, if liked.

Place all the ingredients in a large serving bowl, pour the dressing over, taste, and adjust the seasoning if necessary. Serve immediately.

Serves 4-6

NOTE:

Harissa is a hot North African chili paste, which can be bought from specialty stores. If it is unavailable, hot chili sauce is an alternative.

Broiling these vegetables brings out all their natural flavors, enhancing them with a robust chargrilled taste. Other vegetables that are delicious when cooked this way are onions, plum tomatoes, fennel and endive.

TABBOULEH SALAD

INGREDIENTS

1 cup bulghur wheat
2 cloves garlic, finely chopped
4 tablespoons extra virgin olive oil
juice of 1½ lemons
sea salt and freshly ground black
  pepper
1 ounce flat-leaf parsley leaves
1 ounce mint leaves
4 scallions
1 large plum tomato
1 cucumber
romaine lettuce leaves, parsley and
  mint sprigs to garnish

METHOD

Preparation time: 30 minutes

Place the bulghur wheat in a bowl ad just cover it with boiling water. Set it aside for 20–30 minutes for the grains to swell, and then drain it thoroughly. Place the bulghur wheat in a clean dish towel and squeeze to remove excess moisture. Transfer to a large bowl.

Mix together the garlic, olive oil, lemon juice, salt and pepper. Pour the oily dressing over the bulghur, stir it well, and let stand while preparing the other ingredients.

Coarsely chop the parsley and mint, thinly slice the scallions, and dice the tomato into small chunks. Peel and dice the cucumber. Add the prepared herbs and vegetables to the bulghur. Stir well, and adjust the seasoning if necessary. Transfer the tabbouleh to a serving dish, and serve garnished with romaine lettuce leaves and herb sprigs.

Serves 4

CHICKPEA AND CHORIZO SAUSAGE SALAD

INGREDIENTS

6 ounces raw chorizo sausage
1 tablespoon vegetable oil
2 cups canned chickpeas (garbanzo
  beans)
½ small onion
1 green bell pepper
Vinaigrette:
4 tablespoons light olive oil
1 tablespoon sherry vinegar
2 tablespoons chopped fresh parsley
sea salt and freshly ground black
  pepper
pinch of sugar

METHOD

Preparation time: 20 minutes

Slice the chorizo sausage and fry it with the vegetable oil for about 2 minutes, until it is cooked. Remove it with a slotted spoon and drain on paper towels. Rinse the chickpeas in a colander and drain them.

Slice the onion thinly. Halve the bell pepper, and remove the seeds and core. Cut it into diamond-shaped pieces. Place the vinaigrette ingredients in a screw-topped jar and shake well to combine. Taste and adjust the seasoning if necessary.

Place the chorizo, chickpeas, onion and pepper on a serving plate. Pour the dressing over and toss well to combine. If time permits, let the salad stand for 1 hour before serving to allow the flavors to develop.

Serves 6

Celeriac, Black Bean and Flageolet Salad

INGREDIENTS

½ cup dried black kidney beans
½ cup dried flageolet beans
8-ounce piece celeriac
1 purple onion
Vinaigrette:
3 tablespoons sunflower oil
2 tablespoons red wine vinegar
2 tablespoons sour cream
2 tablespoons chopped fresh thyme
½ teaspoon English mustard
*sea salt and freshly ground black
  pepper*

METHOD

Preparation time: 20 minutes

Soak the beans in separate bowls of cold water overnight, then rinse them and cook them in pans of boiling salted water until they are tender, boiling rapidly for the first 10 minutes. The flageolet beans will take about 40 minutes and the black beans will cook for 1–1¼ hours. Drain the cooked beans and refresh them in cold water, then transfer them to a large bowl and set aside.

Peel the celeriac and cut it into 1-inch cubes. Cook the celeriac in boiling, salted water until it is tender (about 5-6 minutes). Drain and refresh it, and add it to the bowl of beans.

Peel the onion and slice it into thin rings. Add these to the bowl of ingredients. Place all the vinaigrette ingredients in a screw-topped jar and shake well to combine. Taste and adjust the seasoning if necessary, and pour over the beans and celeriac. Toss well to combine and, if time permits, refrigerate the salad for 1 hour before serving to allow the flavors to develop.

Serves 6

– 5 –
SPICY AND EXOTIC

SCALLOP SALAD WITH LIME AND GINGER

INGREDIENTS

16 large scallops with roe
sea salt and freshly ground black
   pepper
2 tablespoons peanut oil
1½ tablespoons finely chopped fresh
   ginger root
1 green chili, seeded and chopped
3 tablespoons fresh lime juice
8 ounces soft lettuce leaves, such as
   Boston or Bibb lettuce
julienne of lime to garnish
Dressing:
6 tablespoons peanut oil
3 tablespoons rice wine vinegar
4 tablespoons chopped fresh
   cilantro
sea salt and freshly ground black
   pepper

METHOD

Preparation time: 25 minutes

Pare some strips of lime zest from the lime and set aside. Separate the roe from the white part of the scallops and halve any large whites. Season well. Heat the oil in a large pan. Add the ginger and chili, and cook for a few seconds. Add the white part of the scallops and cook for about 2 minutes. Add the roe and lime juice, and cook for a further 1–2 minutes. Transfer the contents of the pan to a plate and let cool.

Wash and dry the lettuce leaves, and tear them into bite-size pieces. Place them in a large bowl. Cut fine julienne strips from the reserved lime zest and blanch it for 30 seconds in boiling water. Drain and refresh it in cold water, and set aside.

Place the dressing ingredients in a screw-topped jar and shake well to combine. Taste and adjust the seasoning if necessary. Pour a little of the dressing over the salad leaves and toss gently. Divide the dressed leaves between four plates, and top with the scallops and the roe. Spoon over the remaining dressing; garnish with julienne of lime and serve immediately.

Serves 4

INGREDIENTS

1 butterhead lettuce
2 stalks celery
*1 tangerine and 1 grapefruit or 2 ugli
  fruit*
1 small papaya
*2 teaspoons finely sliced Scotch
  Bonnet (habanero) chili*
Dressing:
1 teaspoon allspice berries
4 tablespoons sunflower oil
1 tablespoon white wine vinegar
1 tablespoon chopped fresh thyme
1 tablespoon papaya seeds
salt and freshly ground black pepper

METHOD

Preparation time: 20 minutes

Remove any damaged, outer leaves from the lettuce and discard them. Wash and dry the remaining leaves, and tear the larger ones into bite-size pieces. Place the lettuce in a large bowl. Slice the celery into thin matchsticks and add these to the lettuce.

Peel the ugli fruit, using a small, sharp knife, and cut in between the membranes to separate the flesh into sections. Add these to the salad bowl. Peel the papaya and halve it. Scoop out the seeds and reserve 1 tablespoon. Cut the flesh into neat chunks and add it to the salad, together with the sliced Scotch Bonnet chilies. (Scotch Bonnet chilies are very hot Jamaican peppers. Always remove the seeds before using, and substitute fresh chilies if they are unavailable.)

Crush the allspice berries in a mortar and pestle, and place them in a screw-topped jar with the other dressing ingredients. Shake well to combine and taste and adjust the seasoning if necessary. Pour the dressing over the salad, toss gently, and serve immediately.

NOTE:
Ugli fruit is a Jamaican citrus fruit, which is a cross between a Seville orange, a tangerine and a grapefruit. 1 tangerine and 1 grapefruit can be substituted.

Serves 4

ROJAK (MALAYSIAN SALAD)

INGREDIENTS

½ small pineapple
1 small cucumber
1 unripe mango
½ cup canned water chestnuts
1 small guava
½ cup bean sprouts
4 ounces yellow-skinned bean curd
vegetable oil for deep-frying
1 tablespoon toasted sesame seeds to
  garnish
(see p.61 for sauce ingredients)

METHOD   Preparation time: 30 minutes

For the sauce, soak the tamarind in ⅔ cup boiling water, breaking up the pulp with a spoon and stirring well. Strain, pressing the pulp against the sieve to extract as much flavor as possible. Discard the dry pulp and reserve the liquid for the sauce.

Place the shrimp paste in a small pan and dry-fry it for 1 minute until it is fragrant. Add the crushed chilies and fry for a further minute. Dry-fry the peanuts in a large skillet, stirring constantly, until they are golden (about 2 minutes). Transfer to a food processor, and dry-fry the sesame seeds for 2 minutes. Add these to the food processor, along with the shrimp paste and chili mixture.

Process the ingredients until finely ground. Add the tamarind liquid and the remaining sauce ingredients, and process again for 1 minute. Transfer the sauce to a pan and cook, stirring occasionally, for 3 minutes. Set it aside to cool.

Peel the pineapple, remove the core, and cut it into neat chunks. Halve the cucumber lengthwise and slice it into diagonal pieces. Peel the mango and cut the flesh into chunks. Halve the water chestnuts lengthwise to produce thin discs. Peel the guava, cut away the seeds, and dice the flesh.

Blanch the bean sprouts for a few seconds in boiling water. Drain and refresh them. Slice the bean curd into small cubes. Deep-fry it in hot oil for about 30 seconds, until it is crisp and golden. Drain it on paper towels.

Arrange all the prepared ingredients in separate groups on a large platter. Spoon some of the sauce into the center of the dish and sprinkle with the toasted sesame seeds. Serve the salad, passing the remaining sauce separately.

Serves 8

Sauce:
1 ounce fresh tamarind
1 tablespoon dry shrimp paste
1 tablespoon crushed dried chilies
1 cup raw unsalted peanuts
¼ cup sesame seeds
juice of 1 lime
1½ teaspoons superfine sugar
1 tablespoon black shrimp paste
1 tablespoon sweet black sauce
pinch of salt

To produce the authentic flavor of this salad, several special ingredients are required. These can be obtained from a good Oriental supermarket. This salad can be served as a first course before an Asian meal.

INGREDIENTS

1 pound cleaned fresh squid
salt and freshly ground black pepper
2 tablespoons peanut oil
10 ounces Chinese cabbage
small handful of cilantro leaves
1 ripe mango
1 green bell pepper
Dressing:
6 tablespoons peanut oil
2 tablespoons lemon juice
2 tablespoons finely chopped shallot
4 teaspoons Thai fish sauce
2 tablespoons chopped fresh cilantro
1 tablespoon chopped fresh mint
2 teaspoons finely chopped red chili
pinch of sugar

METHOD

Preparation time: 25 minutes

Wash and dry the squid, slice it into rings, and season lightly with salt and pepper. Heat the oil in a wok and stir-fry the squid rings until they have turned white and are just cooked (about 5 minutes). Remove them from the wok with a slotted spoon and drain them on paper towels.

Peel the mango and cut the flesh away from the stone. Dice the flesh neatly. Cut the bell pepper in half, remove the core, and slice the flesh into diamonds. Place the ingredients for the dressing in a small bowl and whisk together until thoroughly combined. Taste and adjust the seasoning if necessary. Wash and dry the Chinese cabbage, and break the leaves into bite-size pieces. Place them in a large bowl with the cilantro leaves.

Pour a little of the dressing over the salad leaves, toss well to combine, and line a shallow bowl with the dressed leaves. Place the squid, diced mango and green pepper in a bowl, and pour the remaining dressing over. Toss to combine and spoon the squid mixture onto the salad leaves. Serve immediately.

Serves 4

CREOLE SALAD

INGREDIENTS

1 cup basmati rice
1 eggplant, about 10 ounces
1 tablespoon olive oil
4 ounces cherry tomatoes
1 orange bell pepper
1 small onion
1 cup canned corn
Dressing:
4 tablespoons olive oil
2 tablespoons white wine vinegar
3 tablespoons chopped fresh thyme
2 teaspoons paprika
1 clove garlic, crushed
sea salt and freshly ground black
  pepper

METHOD

Preparation time: 20 minutes

Wash the rice and cook it in boiling salted water until it is tender (about 10–12 minutes). Drain and refresh. Cut the eggplant lengthwise into thick slices and brush both sides with olive oil. Cook the slices under a hot broiler for 6 minutes on each side until crisp and golden. Let cool; then cut them into large dice.

Halve the cherry tomatoes. Halve the bell pepper, remove the core and seeds, and dice the flesh. Peel the onion and slice it thinly. Drain the corn. Place the rice and all the prepared vegetables in a large bowl.

Place the dressing ingredients in a screw-topped jar and shake well. Pour the dressing over the ingredients in the bowl and toss to combine. Taste and adjust the seasoning if necessary and, if time, cover and refrigerate for 1 hour before serving to allow the flavors to develop.

Serves 6

GADOH GADOH (INDONESIAN SALAD)

INGREDIENTS

2 ounces yellow-skinned bean curd
1 ounce raw shrimp crackers
oil for deep-frying
½ cup bean sprouts
2 cups peeled and diced potato
2 ounces Asian long beans or green
  beans
½ cup shredded white cabbage
½ cucumber
1 cup shredded iceberg lettuce
2 hard-boiled eggs, peeled
(see p.65 for sauce ingredients)

METHOD

Preparation time: 30 minutes

Place the first six sauce ingredients in a food processor and blend to a smooth paste. Heat the oil in a saucepan and fry the paste until it is fragrant (about 3 minutes). Crush the peanuts in the food processor and add them to the pan, along with the remaining sauce ingredients. Cook for 4–5 minutes, stirring occasionally. Taste and adjust the seasoning if necessary, and let cool.

Slice the bean curd into thin strips. Deep-fry it in hot oil for 30 seconds until crisp and golden. Remove it with a slotted spoon and drain on paper towels. Deep-fry the shrimp crackers in the hot oil for a few seconds, until they turn white and puff up. Remove them with a slotted spoon and drain on paper towels.

Blanch the bean sprouts for a few seconds in boiling water. Drain and refresh them in cold water. Cook the potato in boiling water until it is tender (about 5 minutes). Drain and refresh it. Cut the beans into 1-inch pieces and blanch them in boiling, salted water. Drain and refresh them.

GADOH GADOH (INDONESIAN SALAD)

Blanch the cabbage for a few seconds. Drain and refresh it. Cut the cucumber into thin slices and, stacking several slices on top of each other, cut across the slices to produce thin "green tipped" strips.

To serve, place the shredded lettuce in a shallow serving dish. Toss together the bean curd, bean sprouts, potato, beans, cabbage and cucumber in a bowl, and spoon this mixture over the lettuce.

Spoon over the peanut sauce, garnish with quartered hard-boiled eggs and slices of chili, and scatter the shrimp crackers on top and around the edges of the bowl. Serve immediately.

Serves 6

Peanut Sauce:
1-inch piece galangal, peeled and
chopped
1 small stalk lemon grass, finely
chopped
1 small red chili, seeded and chopped
1 clove garlic, crushed
2 shallots, peeled and chopped
2 teaspoons dry shrimp paste
2 tablespoons vegetable oil
1 cup salted peanuts
1 tablespoon superfine sugar
1 tablespoon lime juice
2/3 cup coconut milk

Galangal looks similar to ginger root, but the skin is whitish and thinner, tinged with pink. If fresh galangal is unavailable, use the powder version, substituting a teaspoon of powder for the fresh galangal.

ACAR (MALAYSIAN MIXED VEGETABLE SALAD)

INGREDIENTS

4 small carrots
1 large cucumber
1 small cauliflower
4 ounces green beans
8 ounces white cabbage
2 large red chilies
2 large green chilies
10 small shallots
1¼ cups cider vinegar
⅛–¼ cup superfine sugar
3 tablespoons sunflower oil
4 cloves garlic, crushed
1 tablespoon chili powder
1 tablespoon turmeric
½–1 teaspoon salt
1¼ cups salted peanuts
¾ cup toasted sesame seeds

METHOD   **Preparation time:** 25 minutes

Peel the carrots and cut them into thin 2-inch sticks. Cut the cucumber lengthwise into quarters, cut away the seeds, and slice the flesh into thin 2-inch sticks. Divide the cauliflower into florets. Top and tail the beans and halve them. Shred the cabbage finely. Cut the chilies lengthwise into quarters and remove the seeds. Peel the shallots and leave them whole.

Place the vinegar and 1¼ cups of water in a saucepan, and bring to a boil. Blanch the different vegetables in separate batches, cooking each batch for 1-2 minutes, depending on the type of vegetable. Remove each batch with a slotted spoon and place them in a large mixing bowl. Stir in the sugar, and set aside.

Heat the oil in a small pan and fry the garlic until it is golden. Mix the chili powder and turmeric with 2 tablespoons of water to make a paste, and add to the garlic. Cook slowly for about 5 minutes, stirring constantly to prevent the mixture from burning. Stir in the salt and set it aside to cool. Crush the peanuts coarsely, and add to the vegetables with the cooled chili mixture and sesame seeds. Mix well and refrigerate overnight before serving.

Serves 6–8

BOMBAY SALAD

INGREDIENTS

8 ounces broccoli
8 ounces zucchini
½ cup raw cashews
1 tablespoon sunflower oil
¼ teaspoon chili powder
a little sea salt
2 tablespoons coconut flakes
Curry Mayonnaise:
½ cup mayonnaise
1 tablespoon plain yogurt
1 tablespoon mango chutney
2 teaspoons hot curry paste

METHOD

Preparation time: 20 minutes

Divide the broccoli into small florets and cook them in a pan of boiling, salted water for 3 minutes. Drain and refresh them in cold water. Cut the zucchini into 2-inch sticks and cook them in a pan of boiling, salted water for 1–2 minutes. Drain, refresh, and set aside.

Heat the oil in a skillet and stir-fry the cashews for 1–2 minutes until golden. Remove them with a slotted spoon, drain on paper towels, then transfer to a bowl and sprinkle the chili powder and sea salt over the top. Toss well to combine. Dry-fry the coconut flakes for 30 seconds until pale golden. Transfer them to a bowl and let cool.

Place the mayonnaise ingredients in a small bowl and mix well to combine. Place the broccoli, zucchini and half the cashews in a serving bowl. Pour the mayonnaise over and toss gently. Scatter the remaining nuts and the toasted coconut over the top, and serve immediately.

Serves 4

THAI BEEF SALAD

INGREDIENTS

1 pound beef tenderloin
4 ounces baby spinach leaves
8 radishes
4 scallions
1 cucumber
3 tablespoons rice vinegar
4 teaspoons soy sauce
5 tablespoons sunflower oil
pinch of sugar
Marinade:
2 teaspoons chili bean sauce
2 tablespoons Thai fish sauce
juice of 2 limes
1-inch piece fresh ginger root, peeled
  and finely chopped
4 cloves garlic, crushed

METHOD

Preparation time: 30 minutes

Place the marinade ingredients in a small bowl and whisk to combine thoroughly. Wipe the beef and cut it into ½-inch slices. Lay the slices of beef in a shallow glass dish, pour the marinade over, cover, and refrigerate for at least 2 hours.

Crush the garlic and place it in a small bowl. Add the remaining dressing ingredients and mix well to combine. Taste and adjust the seasoning if necessary. Cover the dressing and refrigerate it until required.

Wash the spinach leaves and dry them in a salad spinner. Break off any large stalks and place the spinach in a mixing bowl. Wash the radishes and slice them thinly, then add them to the spinach. Remove the green parts of the scallions and slice the white parts diagonally. Peel the cucumber and dice it. Add these to the bowl, and set aside.

To make garnish tassels, trim away most of the green part of the scallions and discard. With a small pair of scissors, make small cuts from one end of each scallion, about halfway along the length. When they are all cut into fine strips, place them in a bowl of ice-cold water, and refrigerate to allow the ends to curl.

Place the rice vinegar, soy sauce, 4 tablespoons of the sunflower oil, and sugar in a small bowl. Whisk thoroughly to combine and set aside. Remove the beef from the marinade, and heat the remaining sunflower oil in a large pan. Cook the meat in two batches, for 1–2 minutes on each side.

Let the beef stand and then cut it into thin strips. Toss the beef strips in the beef dressing. Add the rice vinegar dressing to the spinach leaves and toss lightly. Line a shallow serving bowl with the dressed spinach. Spoon the beef mixture into the center, garnish with the scallion tassels, and serve immediately.

Serves 4-6

Beef Dressing:
2 cloves garlic
juice 2 limes
2 tablespoons chili sauce
2 teaspoons chopped ginger root
2 teaspoons chopped green chili
4 teaspoons chopped fresh cilantro

CUCUMBER FANS (shown opposite)
Halve a cucumber lengthwise. Place it, cut-side down, on a board and make several fine diagonal cuts in the cucumber, cutting almost to the end of each slice. Bend alternate slices inwards to create loops.

VAN DYKE RADISHES
(shown opposite)
Using a small, sharp knife, make a series of deep zig-zag incisions around the upper edge of each radish. When you have cut all the way around, gently pull apart the two pieces. The tops can also be used for garnishing.

INGREDIENTS

½ cup arame seaweed
1 teaspoon sesame oil
1 cucumber
a little salt
2 ounces daikon (white radish)
2 large carrots
few slices of Japanese pickled ginger
  to garnish
Dressing:
2 tablespoons rice vinegar
2 tablespoons sesame oil
3 teaspoons shoyu (Japanese soy
  sauce)
1 tablespoon sake

METHOD

Preparation time: 25 minutes

Rinse the seaweed and soak it in a bowl of water for 5 minutes. Remove, reserving the water, and sauté the seaweed for 1–2 minutes in the sesame oil. Pour the water into a saucepan, add the seaweed, and simmer, covered, for 35 minutes until it is tender. Drain and set it aside.

Use a citrus stripper to make ridged patterns in the cucumber skin, then slice it very thinly, sprinkle with a little salt, and place it in a colander to remove the moisture. Set aside for 30 minutes. Peel the daikon and slice it thinly on the diagonal. Rinse the cucumber and pat it dry on paper towels.

Peel the carrots and use the citrus stripper to make five ridges along the length of each carrot. Slice the carrots thinly to produce "flowers." Mix the dressing ingredients together until thoroughly combined. To serve, arrange decorative circles of seaweed, carrot, cucumber and daikon on individual plates. Spoon a little dressing over each plate, and garnish each portion with a few slivers of pickled ginger. Serve immediately.

Serves 4–6

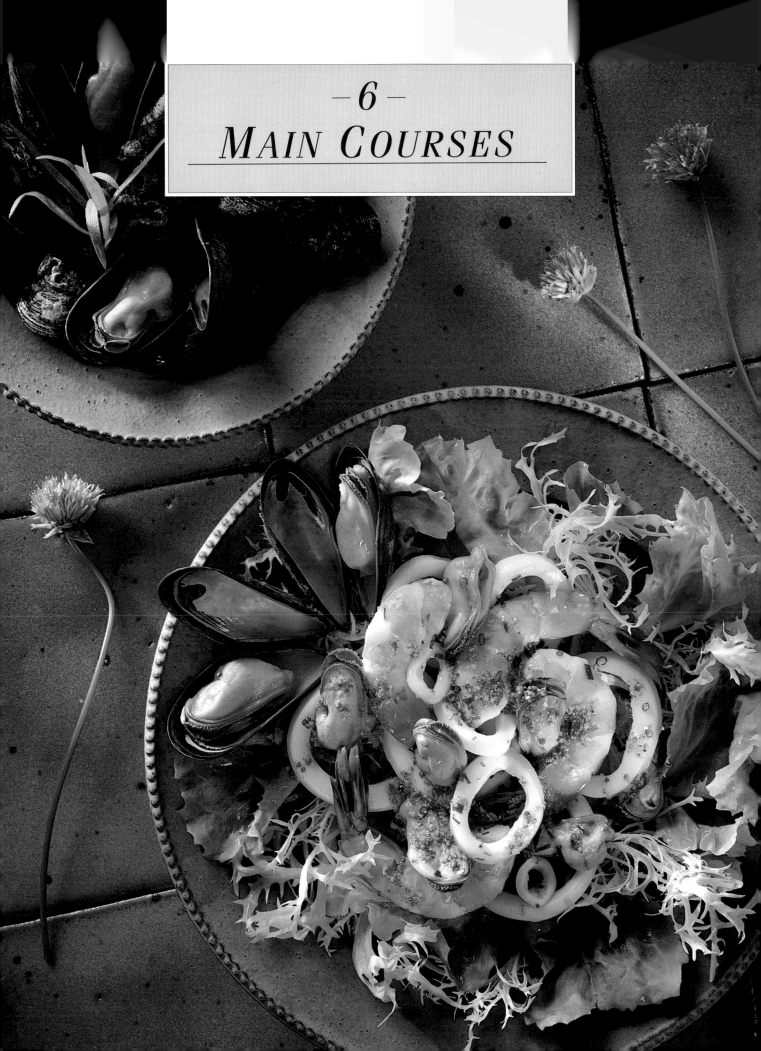

– 6 –
MAIN COURSES

CRISPY DUCK AND MANGO SALAD

INGREDIENTS
....

*2 large Barbary duck breasts, about
    12 ounces each*
1 tablespoon olive oil
1 medium mango, peeled and cubed
¾ cup macadamia nuts
*8 ounces baby spinach leaves,
    washed and dried*
Curried Mayonnaise:
¾ cup mayonnaise
2 teaspoons mild curry paste
1 teaspoon lemon juice
2 tablespoons milk
1 teaspoon mango chutney
salt and freshly ground black pepper

METHOD

Preparation time: 20 minutes
....

Cut each duck breast in half lengthwise and cut each half into thin slices. Heat the oil in a heavy-bottomed skillet and cook the duck strips in two batches, cooking each batch until crisp and golden (about 10 minutes). Remove with a slotted spoon and drain on paper towels. Let cool slightly.

Place all the mayonnaise ingredients together in a bowl and mix well. Season to taste. Just before serving, add the duck strips, mango and macadamia nuts to the mayonnaise. Toss to combine.

Divide the spinach leaves between four large plates and place a quarter of the duck mixture in the center of each plate. Serve immediately.

Serves 4

CHICKEN TIKKA SALAD

INGREDIENTS

1 pound skinned, boned chicken breast
1 romaine lettuce
1 large cucumber, peeled
Tikka Marinade:
1 small onion and 1 clove garlic, chopped
1 tablespoon chopped ginger root
1 teaspoon each of ground coriander,
  ground cumin and garam masala
½ teaspoon salt, turmeric and chili powder
3 tablespoons plain yogurt
2 tablespoons lemon juice
2 tablespoons chopped cilantro
Dressing:
4 tablespoons plain yogurt
2 tablespoons chopped fresh mint
1 tablespoon white wine vinegar
½ teaspoon sugar

METHOD

Preparation time: 25 minutes

Cut the chicken into 1-inch cubes and place in a bowl. Place the marinade ingredients in a food processor and blend to a smooth paste. Toss the chicken cubes in the paste until they are well coated. Cover and refrigerate, preferably overnight, or for several hours before cooking.

Place the dressing ingredients in a small bowl and mix well to combine. Taste and adjust the seasoning if necessary, and refrigerate until needed. Thread the chicken onto 8 skewers and cook under a preheated broiler, turning once, until the chicken is cooked (about 12–15 minutes). Set aside.

Discard any damaged, outer leaves from the lettuce, and wash and dry the remaining leaves. Cut the cucumber in half and use a swivel peeler to produce "ribbons" of cucumber, discarding the central "core" of seeds. Arrange the lettuce leaves and cucumber ribbons on four plates. Place two chicken skewers on each plate and drizzle a little dressing over each portion. Garnish with mint sprigs and serve immediately, passing the extra dressing separately.

Serves 4

AVOCADO SALAD WITH MARINATED PEPPERS

INGREDIENTS

1 pound asparagus
1 small red batavia lettuce or similar
  lettuce
4 marinated bell pepper halves
4 tablespoons walnut pieces
2 large avocados
2 teaspoons lemon juice
focaccia or olive bread to serve
Dressing:
4 tablespoons walnut oil
1 tablespoon red wine vinegar
1 teaspoon French mustard
sea salt and freshly ground black
  pepper
pinch of sugar

METHOD

Preparation time: 30 minutes

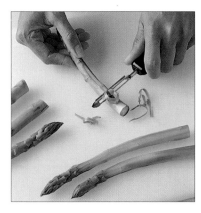

Trim the woody ends from the asparagus stalks and use a vegetable peeler to peel the outer layer of the stalks up to the tips. Cut the asparagus into 2-inch pieces, and blanch them in a pan of boiling, salted water for 2 minutes. Drain and refresh in cold water.

Separate the lettuce into leaves and break into bite-size pieces. Wash the salad and dry it in a salad spinner or between clean dish towels. Drain the bell peppers and cut them into long thin strips.

Toast the walnuts lightly by dry-frying them in a small pan over a medium heat, stirring constantly to prevent them from burning. When they look deep brown (after about 2–3 minutes), transfer them to a plate and let cool.

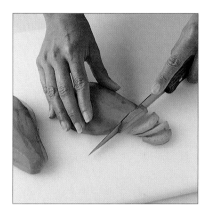

Peel the avocados with a small sharp knife. Halve them and remove the pits. Cut the flesh into thin slices and place them on a large plate. Sprinkle the lemon juice over to prevent discoloration.

Place all the dressing ingredients in a small bowl and whisk together until thoroughly combined. Taste and adjust the seasoning if necessary, and set aside until required.

To serve, divide the lettuce between four plates. Arrange the avocado and asparagus on top of the lettuce, and add some pepper strips to the center of each plate. Scatter the walnuts over the top, spoon some dressing over each salad, and serve immediately with warm bread.

Serves 4

Focaccia is a flat olive-oil bread from Genoa in Italy. It is delicious served with salads, soups, or just eaten on its own. The picture on the right shows plain focaccia, along with two of the flavored versions: onion, and garlic and herb.

INGREDIENTS

2 large freshly-cooked lobsters
1 pink grapefruit
½ ripe peach
½ cup seedless red grapes
3 ounces chicory
Dressing:
1 shallot, finely chopped
1 clove garlic, crushed
2 teaspoons chopped fresh chervil
2 teaspoons chopped fresh tarragon
6 tablespoons light olive oil
2 tablespoons champagne vinegar
sea salt and freshly ground black
  pepper

METHOD

Preparation time: 30 minutes

Remove the lobster heads and break off the large claws. Lay the lobster tail on its back and use scissors or a sharp knife to cut down on either side of the shell. Remove the tail flesh and slice it into thick discs. Crack the claws with a nutcracker and remove the flesh. Cut it into bite-size pieces.

Place all the ingredients for the dressing in a small bowl and whisk to combine. Taste and adjust the seasoning if necessary. Peel the grapefruit with a small sharp knife and divide it into sections, cutting in between the membranes. Slice the peach and halve any large grapes. Wash and dry the chicory.

Divide the chicory between two dinner plates. Arrange the lobster and prepared fruit on the beds of lettuce. Spoon the dressing over each salad, and serve immediately.

NOTE:
Frozen cooked lobster tails can be bought from specialty stores, and are more economical than cooked fresh lobster, but are not, of course, as flavorful.

Serves 2

SMOKED TROUT AND RED BEET SALAD

INGREDIENTS

12 ounces mixed salad leaves, such
  as red loose-leaf, frilice, chervil and
  oak leaf lettuce
6 smoked trout fillets
1½ cups sliced, cooked red beets
shiso or mustard leaves and cress to
  garnish
Dressing:
½ cup sour cream
2 teaspoons horseradish
4 tablespoons virgin olive oil
sea salt and freshly ground black
  pepper

METHOD

Preparation time: 20 minutes

Place all the dressing ingredients in a
small bowl and mix well to combine.
Season to taste and refrigerate to
allow the flavors to develop. Wash
and dry the lettuce leaves, and tear
any large ones into quarters.

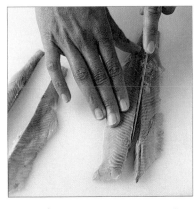

Lay the trout fillets on a board and
divide each fillet in half lengthwise
using a sharp knife.

To serve, divide the salad leaves
between four plates. Arrange three
halves of trout fillet on each plate, and
divide the red beets between the
plates. Spoon over the creamy dressing
and garnish with shiso or mustard
leaves and cress. Serve immediately.

NOTE:
Shiso looks similar to mustard and
cress, except the leaves are purple
and more pointed. It has a mild
"aniseed" flavor.

Serves 4

INGREDIENTS

2 eggs
2 teaspoons vegetable oil
8 ounces smoked tofu
5 ounces oyster mushrooms
1 orange bell pepper
1½ cups sprouted lentils
8 baby corn
1 small lollo rosso loose-leaf lettuce
Dressing:
3 tablespoons peanut oil
1 tablespoon sherry vinegar
1 tablespoon light soy sauce
1 tablespoon chopped fresh ginger
  root
1 scallion, thinly sliced
1 teaspoon clear honey
salt and freshly ground black pepper

METHOD

Preparation time: 30 minutes

Beat the eggs with salt and pepper until well combined. Heat 1 teaspoon of the oil in a skillet and pour in the egg mixture. Cook until it is golden on the underside and cooked in the center. Transfer the omelet to a plate and let cool.

Brush the tofu all over with the remaining teaspoon of oil. Place it under a moderately hot broiler and cook it, turning once, until it is golden (about 10 minutes). Let cool, then slice it into 12 pieces.

Wipe the mushrooms to clean them and slice any that are large. Place them in a large bowl. Halve the bell pepper and remove the core. Cut the flesh into diamond shapes and add these to the mushrooms.

Roll up the omelet and slice it thinly into long strips. Add these to the bowl, along with the sprouted lentils and baby corn, halved lengthwise.

Wash and dry the lettuce leaves and tear them into bite-size pieces. Place all the dressing ingredients in a screw-topped jar and shake well to combine. Taste and adjust the seasoning if necessary.

To serve, divide the salad leaves between four plates. Pour three-quarters of the dressing over the prepared ingredients in the large bowl, and toss lightly to combine. Spoon this mixture over the lettuce, lay three slices of tofu over each portion, and spoon the remaining dressing on top.

Serves 4

VARIATION:

Try varying the flavor of this salad by using the alternative ingredients listed below for the dressing.

3 tablespoons sesame oil
1 tablespoon sherry vinegar
1 tablespoon light soy sauce
1 clove garlic, peeled and finely chopped
1 tablespoon chopped fresh ginger root
1 small green chili, seeded and finely chopped
1 teaspoon clear honey
salt and ground black pepper

GRILLED LETTUCE SALAD

INGREDIENTS

11 ounces mild French goat cheese
4 teaspoons chopped fresh thyme
sea salt and freshly ground black
  pepper
4 crisp lettuce hearts
1 tablespoon olive oil
8 ounces mixed red and yellow
  cherry tomatoes
Dressing:
4 tablespoons olive oil
4 teaspoons white wine vinegar
4 teaspoons Italian black olive paste
salt and freshly ground black pepper

METHOD

Preparation time: 30 minutes

Combine all the dressing ingredients in a small bowl and whisk to combine thoroughly. Season to taste, and set aside. Place the goat cheese and thyme in a small bowl, season with salt and pepper, and mix well to combine. Taste and adjust the seasoning if necessary.

Discard any damaged outer leaves from the lettuces and halve each lettuce lengthwise. Use a small sharp knife to hollow out the heart of each lettuce half. Brush each half with olive oil, and spoon the cheese and thyme mixture into the hollows. Cook under a hot broiler until the cheese begins to brown (about 8–10 minutes), then set aside to cool.

Wash, dry and halve the tomatoes. Divide them between four serving plates. Add two lettuce halves to each plate and drizzle a little of the dressing on top. Spoon the remaining dressing generously over the cherry tomatoes, and serve immediately.

Serves 4

PORK, PRUNE AND PISTACHIO SALAD

INGREDIENTS

4 ounces lollo blondo loose-leaf
   lettuce
1 pint-box shiso
12 ounces pork tenderloin
sea salt and freshly ground black
   pepper
1 tablespoon sunflower oil
4 ounces slim zucchini, halved
   lengthwise
1 tablespoon pistachio nuts
6 ready-to-eat dried prunes,
   quartered
4 dried apricots, cut into slivers
Dressing:
½ teaspoon saffron threads
3 tablespoons plain yogurt
2 tablespoons sunflower oil
2 teaspoons cider vinegar
sea salt and freshly ground black
   pepper

METHOD

Preparation time: 25 minutes

Soak the saffron threads in 2
teaspoons of boiling water and leave
to infuse for 5 minutes. Separate the
lettuce into leaves, and wash and dry
them. Cut the stems of the shiso away
from the roots. Wash and dry the
stems and discard the roots. Place
the dressing ingredients in a bowl and
stir in the saffron threads and water.
Whisk well to produce a smooth
dressing. Taste and adjust the
seasoning if necessary.

Slice the pork into 1-inch pieces and
season it well. Heat the oil, and fry
the pork in two batches until it is
cooked through and golden (about
5 minutes). Transfer to a bowl and
let cool.

Slice the zucchini halves thickly and
blanch them in boiling, salted water
for 1 minute. Drain and refresh them.
Add them to the pork, along with the
pistachios, prunes and apricots. Pour
the dressing over and toss well to
combine. Line a shallow serving bowl
with the lettuce and shiso, and spoon
the pork mixture into the center.
Serve immediately.

Serves 4

INGREDIENTS

20 large raw jumbo shrimp in the shell
2 tablespoons butter
8 ounces mixed salad leaves
1 tablespoon sesame seeds
6 ounces baby corn
1 tablespoon sesame oil
4 bananas
4 tablespoons fresh lime juice
Seasoning:
½ teaspoon salt
2 tablespoons paprika
2 teaspoons cayenne pepper
2 tablespoons dried fines herbes
2 teaspoons garlic flakes
2 teaspoons dried onion flakes
Dressing:
4 tablespoons sesame oil
2 tablespoons fresh lime juice
½ teaspoon sugar

METHOD

Preparation time: 30 minutes

Remove the shells from the shrimp. Using a pair of scissors, cut each shrimp almost in half down to the tail, making sure that it still holds together in one piece. Place the seasoning ingredients in a bowl and mix well to combine.

Melt the butter in a small pan and, using a pastry brush, "paint" each shrimp with butter. Then dip in the seasoning mixture to coat well.

Heat a large cast-iron skillet until it is smoking. Sprinkle a few drops of water onto the surface: if they "dance," it is hot enough to start cooking. Cook the shrimp in three batches, cooking them for 1½–2 minutes on each side until they are "blackened." Set aside to cool.

Wash and dry the salad leaves and herbs. Tear them into bite-size pieces and place them in a large bowl. Dry-fry the sesame seeds in a small pan for 2 minutes, stirring constantly until they are toasted. Transfer them to a bowl to cool.

Blanch the corn in boiling, salted water for 1 minute. Drain them, and then brush them with the sesame oil and sprinkle with sea salt. Cook them under a hot broiler for 5 minutes on each side until lightly charred. Slice the bananas and toss them in the lime juice. Broil them for 3 minutes on each side until lightly charred.

Add the dressing ingredients to the sesame seeds and whisk to combine. Pour the dressing over the salad leaves and toss well. Divide the dressed leaves between four plates. Add five shrimp to each plate, along with a quarter of the chargrilled corn and banana. Serve immediately.

Serves 4

VARIATION:

"Blackening," the method used to cook the shrimp, is a very popular style of cooking in the South. Vary this recipe with "blackened" chicken, using 4 skinless, boneless chicken breasts. Place one chicken breast at a time between sheets of plastic wrap, and beat with a rolling pin until the flesh is about ¼-inch thick. Paint the chicken breasts with melted butter and dip in the spice mixture, as described in the recipe above. Cook the chicken breasts in the same way as the shrimp, but increase the cooking time to four minutes per side.

CRAB SALAD

INGREDIENTS

3 cups fresh white crabmeat
2 large oranges
12 sprigs chervil
2 bunches watercress
20 medium Belgian endive leaves
Dressing:
3 tablespoons crème fraîche
1 tablespoon champagne vinegar
1 tablespoon reserved grated orange
  zest
3 tablespoons grapeseed oil
sea salt and freshly ground black
  pepper

METHOD

Preparation time: 20 minutes

Flake the crabmeat and place it in a bowl. Using a zester, remove 1 tablespoon of zest from one of the oranges and set it aside for the dressing. Then peel both oranges with a small, sharp knife and divide them into sections, cutting in between the membranes. Add the sections to the crabmeat with the chervil sprigs.

Remove any tough stalks from the watercress and break it into bite-size pieces. Wash and dry the watercress and endive leaves, and set them aside.

Place the dressing ingredients in a screw-topped jar and shake well to combine. Taste and adjust the seasoning if necessary. Line a shallow salad bowl with the watercress and endive. Pile the crabmeat and orange mixture into the center, spoon over the dressing, and serve immediately.

Serves 4

ANGLER FISH AND FENNEL SALAD

INGREDIENTS

1 pound 11 ounces angler fish
salt and freshly ground black pepper
2 tablespoons olive oil
2 small red bell peppers
8 cloves garlic, unpeeled
1 pound Florence fennel
1 tablespoon lemon juice
6 ounces escarole lettuce
Dressing:
6 tablespoons olive oil
3 tablespoons balsamic vinegar
2 tablespoons finely chopped fennel
  fronds
sea salt and freshly ground black
  pepper

METHOD

Preparation time: 25 minutes

Remove all the membrane from the angler fish, and cut the flesh away from the central bone. Wash and dry the pieces of fish, season them with salt and pepper, and place them in a small roasting pan with the olive oil. Halve the bell peppers and remove the cores. Place the peppers and the cloves of garlic on a baking sheet. Preheat the oven to 400°F. Bake the fish for about 20 minutes, and the peppers and garlic for about 25 minutes. Remove and set aside to cool.

Remove the fronds from the fennel and reserve for the dressing. Slice the fennel thinly and blanch it for 2–3 minutes in a pan of water, to which the lemon juice has been added. Drain and refresh it in cold water. Place the dressing ingredients in a screw-topped jar and shake well to combine. Season to taste. Wash and dry the lettuce leaves, and tear them into bite-size pieces.

Slice the cooled angler fish into bite-size pieces and place them in a bowl. Cut the peppers into thick strips, removing skins if desired, and add these to the bowl with the fennel. Peel the baked garlic and cut each clove into quarters. Add them to the bowl. Pour the dressing over and toss well to combine. Arrange the lettuce leaves on four serving plates. Divide the fish mixture between the four plates, and serve immediately.

Serves 4

INGREDIENTS

4¼ cups fish stock
2 large sprigs fresh tarragon
8 ounces cleaned squid
16 raw shrimp in the shell
1 pound mussels, scrubbed
6 ounces chicory
6 ounces escarole lettuce
Dressing:
4 tablespoons virgin olive oil
1 tablespoon tarragon vinegar
1 tablespoon chopped fresh tarragon
1 teaspoon snipped chives
2 teaspoons grainy mustard
salt and freshly ground black pepper
pinch of sugar

METHOD

Preparation time: 25 minutes

Place the fish stock and tarragon in a large pan and bring it to a simmer. Slice the squid into rings and poach it in the stock for 2 minutes. Remove with a slotted spoon and set aside. Repeat the process with the shrimp, until the shells turn pink (about 2 minutes), and then with the mussels, until their shells open (also about 2 minutes).

Reserve 8 mussels in their shells. Peel the shrimp and remove the remaining mussels from their shells. Add them to the squid rings. Wash and dry the lettuce, and tear it into bite-size pieces.

Divide the lettuce leaves between four plates. Add a quarter of the mixed seafood to each plate. Place the dressing ingredients in a small saucepan and warm through gently. Spoon the warm dressing over the seafood, garnish each plate with 2 mussels in their shells, and serve immediately.

Serves 4

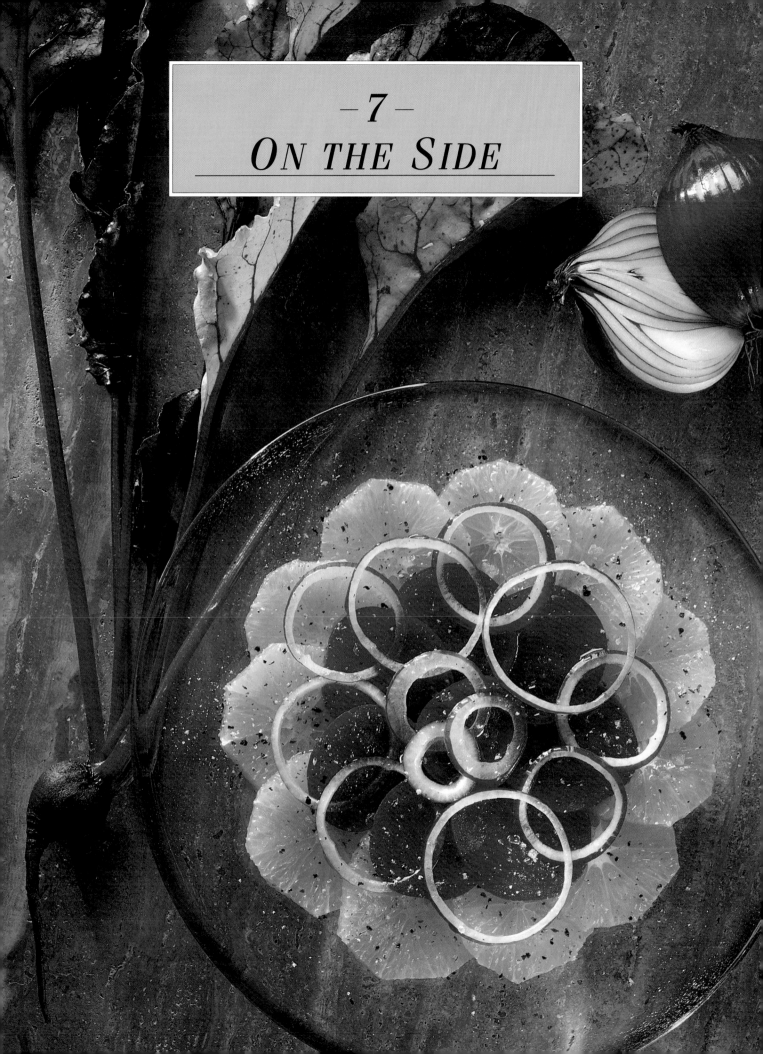

– 7 –
ON THE SIDE

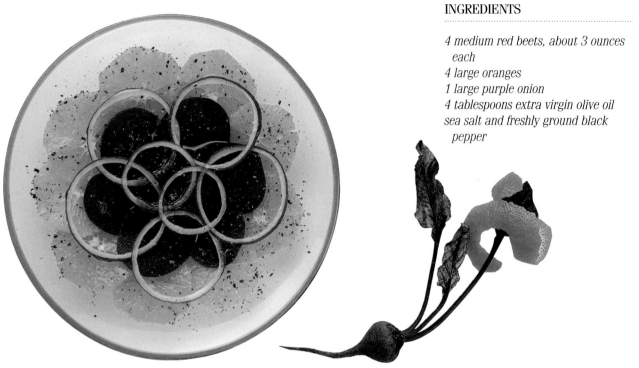

INGREDIENTS

*4 medium red beets, about 3 ounces
  each*
4 large oranges
1 large purple onion
4 tablespoons extra virgin olive oil
*sea salt and freshly ground black
  pepper*

METHOD

Preparation time: 20 minutes

Remove any leaf stalks from the beets, but do not trim off the tapering roots. Wash them carefully, taking care to keep the skins intact so they do not "bleed" while cooking. Cook in salted water until they are tender (about 1-1½ hours). When the beets are cool, peel off their skins.

Using a small sharp knife, remove the skin and pith from the oranges. Slice each orange thinly into rings. Peel the onion and slice it thinly. Separate the slices into rings.

To serve, slice each beet and arrange on a plate with one of the sliced oranges. Scatter some onion rings over each portion and drizzle 1 tablespoon of olive oil over the top. Season generously with salt and pepper, and serve immediately.

NOTE:
To save time, the red beets can be bought ready-cooked and peeled from most large supermarkets. Allow about 3 ounces per person.

Serves 4

AVOCADO AND WATERCRESS SALAD

INGREDIENTS

2 bunches watercress
2 avocados
1 tablespoon lemon juice
Dressing:
1 lemon
6 tablespoons grapeseed oil
1 teaspoon Dijon mustard
½ teaspoon clear honey

METHOD

Preparation time: 15 minutes

Using a zester, pare 1 teaspoon of lemon zest from the lemon and reserve it. Squeeze the juice and place all the dressing ingredients in a screw-topped jar. Shake well to combine. Taste and adjust the seasoning, adding more honey if necessary, then set aside.

Remove any thick stalks and the roots from the watercress. Break the leaves and young stalks into small bite-size pieces, and wash and dry them. Peel the avocados, halve them, and remove the pits. Then slice them thickly and place in a small bowl with the lemon juice to prevent discoloration.

To serve, place the avocado and the watercress in a salad bowl, pour the dressing over and toss gently to combine. Scatter the reserved lemon zest on top, and serve the salad immediately.

Serves 4

BEAN AND PEA SALAD

INGREDIENTS

6 ounces thin green beans
14-ounce can petits pois
3 scallions
Garlic Mayonnaise:
½ cup mayonnaise
1 clove garlic, crushed
2 tablespoons chopped fresh parsley
2 tablespoons milk
½ teaspoon sea salt
½ teaspoon superfine sugar
freshly ground black pepper

METHOD

Preparation time: 25 minutes

Top and tail the beans, and cut them into 1-inch pieces. Cook them in a pan of boiling, salted water until they are cooked but still crisp (about 5 minutes). Drain and refresh them in cold water, and place them in a large bowl.

Drain the petits pois and add them to the beans. Wash and trim the scallions, and slice them thinly on the diagonal. Add these to the bowl.

Place all the ingredients for the garlic mayonnaise in a small bowl and mix well to combine. Taste and adjust the seasoning if necessary. Add the mayonnaise to the peas and beans, and toss until all the vegetables are well coated. Transfer to a serving bowl and, if time permits, let stand for 30 minutes to allow the flavors to develop.

Serves 4

CARROT AND DAIKON SALAD

INGREDIENTS

12 ounces carrots
12 ounces daikon (white radish)
4 tablespoons raisins
Vinaigrette:
1 tablespoon cumin seeds
4 tablespoons sunflower oil
4 teaspoons rice wine vinegar
½ teaspoon chili powder
sea salt and freshly ground black
  pepper

METHOD

Preparation time: 25 minutes

Trim the ends from the carrots and daikon, and peel them. Using a swivel vegetable peeler, shave long "ribbons" from the carrots and daikon, and place them in a bowl. Stir in the raisins and set aside.

Dry-fry the cumin seeds in a small pan for 1–2 minutes, until they begin to "pop." Then transfer them to a small bowl and add the remaining vinaigrette ingredients.

Whisk together until thoroughly combined. Taste and adjust the seasoning if necessary, and pour the dressing over the carrot and daikon. Toss well to combine and, if time permits, let stand for 30 minutes to allow the flavors to develop.

NOTE:
Try adding 2 tablespoons of pistachio nuts to this salad for an interesting variation.

Serves 6

SPRING SALAD

INGREDIENTS

6 ounces mixed green salad leaves,
  such as romaine, chicory and oak
  leaf lettuces
2 ounces snow peas
½ large green bell pepper
2 stalks celery
basil sprigs to garnish
Fresh Herb Dressing:
4 tablespoons olive oil
4 teaspoons champagne vinegar
1 tablespoon chopped fresh parsley
1 tablespoon chopped fresh basil
1 tablespoon chopped fresh chervil
sea salt and freshly ground black
  pepper
pinch of sugar

METHOD

Preparation time: 20 minutes

Wash and dry the salad leaves, and tear them into bite-size pieces. Place them in a large bowl. Top and tail, and halve, the snow peas. Blanch them in boiling, salted water for 30 seconds, drain and refresh them under cold water, and add them to the lettuce leaves.

Remove the core from the bell pepper, and slice into long thin strips. Slice the celery on the diagonal, and add both of these to the bowl of salad leaves.

Place the dressing ingredients in a screw-topped jar and shake well to combine. Toss the dressing through the salad, and serve immediately in individual bowls, garnished with a sprig of basil.

Serves 4

SALAD LEAVES WITH ROASTED PEPPER DRESSING

INGREDIENTS

20 medium Belgian endive leaves
12 medium radicchio leaves
3 hard-boiled eggs, peeled and sliced
12 black olives
Pepper Dressing:
1 medium red bell pepper, quartered
1 large red chili
1 tablespoon olive oil
1 small shallot, chopped
1 clove garlic, chopped
2 tomatoes, skinned, seeded and
    chopped
2 tablespoons mayonnaise
sea salt and freshly ground black
    pepper

METHOD

Preparation time: 30 minutes

Place the bell pepper and chili under a hot broiler for 10–15 minutes until charred on all sides. Let cool, then remove the skins and seeds, and chop the flesh roughly.

Heat the olive oil in a skillet. Add the shallot and garlic and cook for 3–4 minutes, then add the tomatoes and cook for a further 2 minutes until the mixture is soft. Let cool, and then place in a food processor together with the pepper and chili, and blend to a smooth puree. Add the mayonnaise, salt and pepper, and blend again briefly. Taste and adjust the seasoning if necessary.

To serve, wash and dry the salad leaves and divide them between four plates. Spoon the dressing over and top with slices of egg and the olives.

Serves 4

POTATO, MUSHROOM AND CUCUMBER SALAD

INGREDIENTS

1 pound baby new potatoes
8 ounces brown button mushrooms
1 cucumber
Mustard Mayonnnaise:
4 tablespoons mayonnaise
4 tablespoons crème fraîche
2 teaspoons grainy mustard
sea salt and freshly ground black
  pepper
pinch of sugar

METHOD

Preparation time: 20 minutes

Scrub the potatoes and cook them in a pan of boiling, salted water until they are tender (about 12 minutes). Drain and refresh them under cold water, and slice each potato in half. Place them in a large bowl. Wipe and trim the mushrooms, and halve any that are large. Add them to the potatoes.

Peel the cucumber and halve it lengthwise. Using a teaspoon, scoop out the seeds and slice the flesh into half-moon shapes. Add to the potatoes and mushrooms. Place the ingredients for the mayonnaise in a bowl and mix well to combine.

Add the mayonnaise to the potatoes, mushrooms and cucumber, and toss well to ensure that everything is well coated. Taste and adjust the seasoning if necessary, then let stand for 1 hour before serving to allow the flavors to develop.

Serves 6

INGREDIENTS

8 ounces mixed salad leaves
Dressing:
2 anchovy fillets, finely chopped
2 tablespoons chopped fresh
* tarragon*
1 tablespoon snipped fresh chives
1 tablespoon chopped fresh parsley
²/₃ cup mayonnaise
1 tablespoon tarragon vinegar
1 tablespoon water
sea salt and freshly ground black
* pepper*

METHOD

Preparation time: 15 minutes

Place the chopped anchovy fillets in a bowl with the herbs, mayonnaise, vinegar and water, and mix well to combine. Season lightly with salt (the anchovies are salty) and black pepper.

Wash the salad leaves and dry them in a salad spinner. Tear the larger leaves into bite-size pieces.

Toss together the salad leaves and dressing in a large bowl, and serve immediately on individual plates.

Serves 4